Tim Low

Millionaire

Mindset

A Decade of Distilled Wit &
Wisdom from the Outspoken
UK Marketer...

By Tim Lowe

Tim Lowe's Millionaire Mindset

Published by Waverley Media Ltd
Waverley Farm
Waverley Lane
Farnham
GU9 8EP

ISBN 978-0-9928441-0-3

Contents

Know what you want!

It's my first week back after a very long Christmas holiday so, firstly, I hope that you had a really enjoyable Christmas and are going to have a truly prosperous New Year!!!

I know that I had a fantastic time throughout December and the first few days of January.

Now this is not, as many people might suspect, because I have excessive amounts of free time and money (any spare cash is immediately "hoovered" up by my wife and they can always find me plenty of "little jobs" to do just when I am contemplating a nice snooze on the sofa).

The biggest single reason that I had such a great time is because, and please don't dismiss this:

I knew exactly what I wanted. All year I was focused on my goals, one of which was how I wanted to spend December.

This may sound a bit obsessional but in reality if you set out on a journey with nowhere in mind that is exactly where you will end up.

I got exactly what I wanted simply because I knew the tiniest details of my objectives and everything I did was geared towards getting them.

Incidentally my objectives for last year were not just to have a month's holiday at Christmas!! I had lots of other goals too, it's just the holiday one is a good example.

The best way to get what you want is to know exactly what it is that you are aiming for, write it down and plan how to get there. Quite literally, I have a wall planner on which I work out the timings for everything that I want to do and a very definite list of objectives, both business and personal.

I am not suggesting that I or anybody else, will always achieve every single objective but at least I know where the target is and hit it 97 times out of a hundred!

So instead of a snooze, try a goal list instead.

10th January 2004

There is always a new niche opening up that somebody is going to exploit – make sure that it's you.

My Dad came to visit me today and as he watched me answering some emails he asked what exactly it is that I do to earn a living! Since he is 69 my answer involved me attempting to explain what the internet really is, he has heard of it, even seen it but is not entirely certain "what" it is.

This got me thinking that although many people now rely on it for all manner of things (including the manufacturers of my wife's digital camera who are so sure that we all have a connection that they don't bother with an instruction book, instead putting one online) in reality it has only been around, commercially, for about 6 or 7 years.

Certainly I only got a connection in 1999 but feel as though I have had it all my life. It's hard to believe that something that is so recent allowed me to bring in about 600,000 pounds last year – and still work from home.

Anyway, the point is that my Dad said something like "well you found a niche and exploited it, but is it still there?"

Apart from the fact that it obviously still is, since last year I did more than 3 times what I did the year before, it doesn't actually matter.

The whole internet wasn't there until a few years ago, in fact when I left school (not that long ago, I'm 39) Personal Computers were just about a reality and Microsoft weren't yet even in business so I'm quite certain that other markets and niches will open up every day for as long as any of us will live.

Frankly I would not be bothered if the internet evaporated tomorrow, I know that in no time at all something else would come along that could be exploited just as easily.

The moral is "Carpe Diem" (Seize the Day) and don't let worry about the good times ending stop you taking advantage of them when they do arrive.

17th January 2004

Fiscal Prudence is the way to ensure a stress free and ultimately profitable business AND home life.

What on earth do I mean by fiscal prudence?

I have a phrase that makes my wife cringe every time I say it – "if your outgoings exceed your income, your upkeep will be your downfall".

No matter what my circumstances (I have in the past been very poor and spent an unhappy 6 months on the dole) I never spend more than I earn and generally quite a bit less.

In fact, I make it my goal to spend no more than half of what I earn (although 'She Who Must...' has a jolly good try at exceeding this level).

I am not saying that it is easy to never run up debts. It is not very hard to get into debt but believe me it is even harder to pay those debts once you have them.

For a start if you pay by credit card and choose to take say 2 years to pay for an item you are probably paying at least 30% extra for the same thing.

How much of a bargain was it to buy that irresistible item in the sales because it had 20% off?

Secondly your monthly disposable income is continually shrinking. You are far better off saving for an item than using credit. Often if you pay by cash you can get a better price as well.

If you must pay for something on credit "now" then either pay for it as quickly as you can i.e. pay every spare penny to your debt to get rid of it so you pay as little interest as possible; or better yet find some alternative way of funding it – for example, if it's a business deal and you cannot find the money take on a partner (no, not me I have that request about 50 times a week already).

This has the added advantage that you have somebody else's ideas and skills to help you succeed as well.

24th January 2004

Be Prepared to be Ignored and Doubted.

Human beings are funny creatures, they resemble ostriches in some ways. No I have not lost my few remaining marbles, I am musing on some people's reaction to last week's tip.

You may recall that I banged on about fiscal prudence, sadly not a popular topic!

Some weeks I can send out these tips and get zero unsubscribe requests but on the weeks where I cover "uncomfortable" subjects like saving money instead of spending it or working instead of watching soap operas I always get a little crop of people unsubscribing and a few half-wits emailing me with complaints about my views.

Do I care? Why should I? Have these people cost me anything? No. Have they cost themselves anything?

Almost certainly!

It's the same when I make an offer to my potential customers. Some buy, some don't and some whinge about it.

I am afraid that a person has to get used to it. Any business is rather like panning for gold, you have to sift out all the bits of clinker and worthless rubbish to find the odd nugget. Lots of little nuggets add up to a pot of gold. (I'm rather pleased with that analogy but as 'She Who Must...' says "I would need to be".)

The trick is to keep panning, the more you pan the more nuggets you will find.

This principle overcomes the other thing that has amazed me this week:

It is frankly astonishing how you can send somebody a letter 3 or 4 times and they will call and ask why you have only just told them about something! What happened to the first 3 letters?

The Postman ate them perhaps? They were abducted by aliens then? No.

People just weren't in the right frame of mind the day that they got them so they ignored them.

So keep panning!!

31st January 2004

Good Products often come out of Necessity.

Later this year I am going to be hosting a workshop for budding entrepreneurs who want to use their websites to maximum effect without bothering too much with what I now think of as "traditional" tools such as Search Engines.

To do this I was collecting together all the bits and pieces that I use every day to run my business and realised that I had developed, or to be precise, caused to be developed (by my longer suffering technical wizard – Dr Henry) quite a lot of really good stuff that other people will want.

For example I have a gadget that tells me how far a visitor got into reading one of my websites before they left. If I know that a lot of people leave at a certain point then I can try and get them past that point by changing the text.

Similarly I have a password control system that restricts access to parts of my system so that only people who I choose can see certain special offers.

I realised that I had 8 really top products, that people pay hundreds of pounds a year to use from other suppliers, just sat there making my life easier but not making any money.

All they needed was a nice interface for the customer to use and they were ready to sell.

You may often find that you have made something that helps you, but that other people would be quite happy to pay you for.

It is certainly worth looking at how you do things and seeing if you have any "diamonds in the rough" sat around gathering dust!

21st February 2004

Creating a Mastermind Group Will Quadruple or More Your Ideas and Productivity

It can be a lonely life running your own business, especially if those around you do not always support what you are doing.

Firstly if someone is negative then learn to tune them out or don't talk to them. If it's a husband or wife this can be difficult so try to "agree to differ", if you can't then get a new partner (for some reason I always get in trouble for this sort of comment, oh well!)

However what you really need are people around you who don't necessarily agree with everything you say but who will offer constructive help.

Ideally you need a small "Mastermind Group".

I am not talking about people sat in black chairs (showing my age now) but people with whom you can brainstorm ideas because they think along similar lines to you.

There is a lot of tosh talked "brainstorming" so let me give you an example of how this should really work.

I have a friend who is in a similar business that I talk to most days, he sends me his new ideas and I send him mine.

We will then work through them over the phone or get together one evening if we need to (for instance if he wanted me to watch a tape). When we work on these ideas quite literally he will explain his thinking and I will make comments and suggest additions as he talks. He will do the same for me.

On Thursday we talked for 5 hours straight! By the time we had finished our plans were entirely different and a whole lot better plus we had developed enough new ideas that just popped up to last the rest of the year.

I would never have got my plans so well refined and likely to succeed without this process.

I have a similar arrangement for working with Henry who does all my technical stuff, when I can persuade him to talk to me (he is often lost in a world all of his own) nearly always the whole is much more than the sum of the parts.

However, beware, this only works if your chosen Mastermind people are "on your wavelength". If they are not then you will have a stilted one-sided conversation with someone that will get you nowhere. It could be that your husband or wife are not on your wavelength when it comes to business so choose carefully, but when you get it right it's well worth the effort.

6th March 2004

Keep your sail up and when the wind blows your boat will move!

If your sail is stowed away waiting until conditions are perfect then when you eventually get it out the wind may have passed.

You may be forgiven for thinking that that my marbles have once again been mislaid. (A permanent state of affairs according to 'She Who Must...'.)

What I am getting at is that many people are not at all ready to do business when the opportunity arises. They think that they are looking seriously for their chance to come but in reality they turn down or don't recognise every chance they get.

And often when they do take that chance they have waited so long that it is way too late.

My advice is to have that sail up at all times, always be ready for a gust of wind, it may only move you a little way forward but at least you are moving, not moored up bemoaning the lack of perfect weather!

The serious entrepreneur will make decisions quickly and get doing. I know that for many years I was convinced that I was going to "do something" but just never did, probably 11 or 12 years passed whilst I was "thinking about it", "looking around" or "researching". Yeah right!

Is this you too?

Now I really do try to make things happen whilst they are fresh in my mind. don't always succeed but I do about 70% of the time which is enough for a pretty nice business.

3rd April 2004

How to avoid paying people to work for you but still keep them happy!

By and large I never pay for anything important from anybody on a straight forward "they sell – I pay" basis.

'She Who Must...' has just pointed out that I am notoriously mean but that isn't fair (I have to be anyway to make way for a certain amount of spending).

I am not mean ... I just like value for money.

What I do is pay on results. You cannot do this with everything of course. Nobody will sell you envelopes on this basis, nor will Bill Gates sell you Windows software this way either but I would not pay a decorator to paint my house until he's done it.

The difference here is that something like decorating is a skill which the man has yet to exercise and the same goes for things like website designers and sales copywriters.

I always aim to pay a more than fair price, based on what their work produces. I do the same with people who ask me to market their products, I will not usually buy the rights to that product but I will sell it on a joint venture basis.

Obviously there are exceptions to this. If I know the guy whose product it is and I know he is good then it is often cheaper to just buy the rights.

The other exception is where the end result is in somebody else's control. Imagine that I offered my decorator a percentage of the increase in value of my house after he'd decorated it, but I get to choose the decoration.

A silly example but the point it makes is that clearly he might lose out because I had chosen poorly, which would not be fair.

So it goes for technical people and copywriters, I simply pay them a small percentage of what they help me make, but I give them control of their part of the project so if it's wrong then it's their problem not mine. Conversely when everything works well then they earn much more than they would otherwise have done.

In this way I have got most projects off the ground without spending hardly any money at all!

5th June 2004

How to treble your profits by relaxing.

Regular readers will remember that I bought a spa bath for my garden a couple of weeks ago, you may also recall that I was unconvinced that I needed one.

In fact I had it installed as part of a complete re-landscaping and improvement of my garden. I have gone from having one huge patch of grass with the odd flower bed around the edges and a BBQ area to a number of completely different and separate themed "rooms".

I use different parts depending upon my mood and have entertaining and business areas that are separate (I have an office in the garden so I sometimes have business meetings outside).

Why on earth am I telling you about my garden?

Well I would not have believed it possible but spending a bit of time and effort separating my business and personal areas and relaxing in the spa bath has had an enormous effect on my business output.

I am normally unable to get to sleep easily and often lay awake all night thinking about all the things that I haven't got done. When I wake up I often feel tired before I start to do anything. The spa has changed all that.

I go in just before bed and relax totally, I am asleep almost as soon as I go to bed and wake feeling ready for anything.

After 40 years I have eventually found something that helps me sleep!

No, I am not saying that everybody needs a spa bath to make it in business. But what I am saying is that if you do whatever you need to do so that you can relax and be creative then you will experience a huge increase in your effectiveness.

I've created more new projects in 2 weeks that I have in the past 12 months, without really trying. I just wish that I'd bought a spa 10 years ago!

7th August 2004

How to pick the best places to advertise your business or product every single time.

My original headline for this tip read - If you do what everybody does, you'll get what they get. Here's what I mean:-

This is good and bad. For example: If you get a job as a waiter and do what all the other waiters do, in the same way as they do, then you'll get no more or no less tips than they get. If you are a bit less attentive and a bit less interested then you'll get less tips, however if you are a bit more pleased to see people and look after them a little better then you can expect a few more tips.

As usual, about now you probably imagine the Timmy marbles have gone AWOL (its age I think) but stay with me on this.

Now imagine you were a really good waiter that was looking for a new place to work. If you went and worked in a restaurant that had just opened in a side street that nobody walked down, then no matter how good you were, you would not earn as many tips as a mediocre waiter working in a busy place with a queue out the door.

I'm nearly there! Now think of yourself as a hungry person in an unfamiliar town looking for somewhere to eat, you stop the car and ask a passerby where to get some food – the chances are that he will say something like "all the restaurants are down that way".

So that is where you go, to a place where there are lots of what you are looking for.

So it is with advertising. If you place ads where everybody else does then that is, where potential customers know to look (you wouldn't advertise your car for sale in a gardening magazine would you?).

Competition here is much less of a problem than being the only advertiser, realistically if there is only your ad who is going to see it unless it's huge? Whereas everybody knows that cars are advertised on Thursdays in such and such paper and jobs are Tuesdays etc.

So my waiter should get a job in a restaurant that is near all the other eateries (advertise where all your competitors do because undoubtedly that is what works). Then the attentive waiter will get a lot of the attention and business (i.e. just make your ad a little better than everybody else's).

A mediocre ad in the right place will outperform the best ad in the world if it's placed somewhere that nobody looks.

Never be tempted to be the first to advertise somewhere, let others do that and just keep a watchful eye on where "all" the other businesses regularly advertise.

14th August 2004

Success is in the details...

Yesterday I was picking up a Dinner Suit from an outfitters which I usually call "Bruce the Cloth" for a function I'm going to this evening.

Brucie has been supplying me with suits, shirts, trousers etc for some years and knows my sizes and preferences as well as I do, probably better in fact – if I want something in particular I don't bother looking around, trudging from shop to shop. I just call Bruce and he gets it.

We have an understanding on pricing and generally everything works out very well.

When he had pinned the trousers up so that his seamstress could take them up he mentioned that I had left the shoes that I was going to wear with the suit in the changing rooms.

"Of course I have, so that I can try the trousers on when Barbara has taken them up" said I.

He laughed and seemed to find this amusing, I asked him what was funny and he told me that my behaviour was "endearing" – I think he meant "bloody annoying" actually!

Despite the fact that he has altered many pairs of trousers for me I still needed to check, which he found "endearing", he said that 98% of his customers would just trust him.

And so would I, to do his best or not to overcharge, but I also know that he and the rest of us are human and make errors – not intentionally but by mistake. No matter how careful or trustworthy somebody is, we all make mistakes.

Whilst I was waiting for the alterations I tried on some shorts and said that I would have 3 pairs, I tried all 3 pairs on – much to Bruce's amusement. Then he remembered that once before I had not done so, only to find that one pair was wrongly marked. It takes 3 minutes to try them on but an hour and a half round trip to take them back if they don't fit.

So it is with websites, forms that you fill in and every other aspect of your business. It pays huge dividends to check every single link on a site, every spelling several times and every bit of functionality several times on several different computers.

You would be amazed at how many mistakes you will find every time you check the same thing in your business or on your website. Every mistake could be lost revenue, personally I hate wasted time and I hate lost revenue even more.

4th September 2004

You never know the outcome until you try so test, test and test some more!

This week I have sent out two different offers to two groups of people.

I had sent both offers before and thought that I knew what the outcome would be so felt confident to change one or two minor things in the presentation, and I do mean MINOR.

I changed things like envelope colour and font, really trivial stuff.

Based on past experience of both groups and what has worked before I thought that I could predict the result.

I was wrong, both times (I'm always wrong if 'She Who Must...' is to be believed, bless her, she's just walked into the room and given me my daily list of things I have done wrong already!).

Anyway, I expected a low priced offer that I had sent to pull in a huge response and I expected a more expensive offer to do okay but not pull in massive numbers. Well, the low priced offer bombed (I say bombed – has sort of broken even) and the more expensive one has pulled in more than twice what I was expecting.

It is tempting to look at what I did on the expensive one and hold this up as the magic formula but sadly, this isn't the case. In reality "the magic formula" is slightly different for each group of people. The

29

basics are the same but you have to test all sorts of variables based on nothing more than gut instinct to get to the optimum response for that particular group of people.

So the moral is if you change anything at all either on a website or in letters that you send to customers, you need to test the result against previous results and see you have improved the situation or made it worse.

25th September 2004

Whether you think that you can or whether you think that you can't – you're quite right.

The vast majority of people don't believe in themselves, they maintain that there is some special reason why other people who succeed have done so and that: "it's alright for them, they had it easy because......"

By contrast successful people simply know that if they keep trying they will find a way of making things work.

When I first started my business I used to advertise my websites in national newspapers .

Often things would not go how I expected but I used to look at other ads that had been running for years and say to myself that if it didn't make money for those guys then they wouldn't keep advertising, would they?

Slowly but surely, I worked out how to make money this way ... and 4 years on (nearly) I do very well.

Just recently I have shared that experience with some people and I have been amazed at the variation in what people have achieved using it.

Some, the majority in fact have done nothing at all – this is not really surprising – most people don't get around to doing things or get distracted quite easily.

Another group give up at the first hurdle – rather like the smoker trying to quit who rips off his patches and lights up after only a few days when he is under stress. (Yes, I did give up years ago and yes, reformed smokers are the worst kind!)

A third group make a valiant effort but become depressed when their first ad fails and then quit.

Only about 2% of people look at a failed ad as nothing more than part of learning what works, rather like falling off a bicycle the first time you ride one.

The most amazing thing is that some of the people who give up early then look at what they are doing and say "this idea doesn't work" – despite the obvious contradiction that it does work for me and just as importantly it does work for that 2% of others as well.

 The difference between the 2% who make it work and the 98% who don't is simply that the 2% believe in themselves and persevere whereas the 98% convince themselves that it is somebody else's fault or that the system is broken.

I have run loads of ads that haven't worked, but overall when I have got it right then I have cleaned up.

If you want to succeed you need to be one of the 2% of people who take responsibility, believe in themselves and learn from their actions and results whatever the outcome.

31st October 2004

How many people have you confused this week?

Yesterday I was speaking at a workshop and was quite surprised at the number of people who cornered me at lunchtime to explain that they didn't think that they could do as I was suggesting because it was too "hard" and they were going home (I always offer the option to leave at lunchtime and get any payment back).

This was very unusual because I have made the same recommendations many times without incident.

It turns out that I had chosen to explain things without the slide that I normally use and, without thinking, I used words that are "insider terms".

The sad thing is the people who were telling me that they were leaving were in fact perfectly capable of following the instructions they were given but were uncomfortable with the idea of saying that they didn't understand me and "looking stupid" so they would sooner make an excuse and scuttle off home.

When I discovered this and explained a bit more clearly at least half of them suddenly changed their minds and stayed, which is good for them (and good for me of course).

So this morning I had a wander around some of my websites and some other people's and was horrified at how complicated we make some things for people who are new to navigating around websites and the internet, equally we often use words that are impenetrable to most potential customers.

My mistakes have cost me thousands so always use language that your customers understand and save some of those lost sales.

6th February 2005

It often doesn't take much to "clean up" by being streets ahead of your competitors and NOT offering what you think people want...

I have just spent the weekend being dragged (by 'She Who Must...') around bathroom emporiums.

We have been everywhere from cheap and cheerful warehouses full of plastic baths to super posh showrooms selling baths costing £7,500 and taps for another couple of thousand!

Needless to say we have yet to find anything that is suitable.

However, everywhere we went I would try and find a sales person and would enquire if they could just pop round, measure up and suggest what would look nice and fit in the room. Almost all said that they did not offer this service and left it at that (including the one with the baths costing as much as a car).

Eventually one posh place said they did "design" for a charge.

They are coming Wednesday and unless they are completely useless guess who is getting to supply my bathroom?

The next thing was installation. Again, all most of them wanted to do was sell the kit and leave me to worry about fitting it. I saw hordes of bewildered people being told that it "wasn't cost effective" for the supplier to design the bathroom or actually fit it. The customer should make their own arrangements.

Again the bods coming on Wednesday will install, by now I really don't care if they are more expensive than anybody else, I will just be grateful that somebody else is going to worry about the details!

Whatever your business, the chances are that your competitors are running their operation for their own convenience, not the customers.

These days people are overawed by choice and have far too much information, all they really want is to get to where they want to be, which in my case was with a new bathroom.

You can be more expensive and have a more limited offering but if it is more convenient for your customer they will buy from you almost every time. In other words give customers what they want (try asking them what that is) rather than what you think they want.

27th February 2005

Get a bucket and sponge and wash your garage doors! Your sales will definitely improve.

A very good friend of mine used to sell new houses and tells this story. He and his colleagues used to occupy the show house waiting for potential customers to come calling, often they would wonder why things were a little slower than they were expecting and would try and work out what was "wrong".

One chap's solution was always to go and straighten all the furniture and give the windows and doors a good clean, he felt that the garage door in particular needed to be sparkling clean in order for passers-by to be enticed in to take a closer look. Apparently whenever he went and washed the garage doors he would sell more houses.

I find the same thing works in my business, if we are sending out a mail shot, even though I have built up a little team of trusted people to stuff all the envelopes and stick the stamps on etc., quite often I will personally go and check that every single letter has a stamp and will count them and open a few to see that they are correct.

I will generally find only the odd mistake but more importantly the people know that I am going to do this from time to time so they do a better job. For a while I stopped bothering and gradually results slipped, as soon as I started checking again the results improved.

By the way, if you are tempted to think that checking people's work will demoralise them, then you may be right if they are slackers. But if they strive to do a perfect job they will welcome you finding out that they have done well, after all what would be the point of trying really hard if nobody ever knew or said "thank you and well done".

Being personally involved and just ensuring that the details are perfect will pay dividends, every time.

5th March 2005

5th March 2005

What do you cost per hour?

A few years ago now 'She Who Must...' convinced me to get a lady to do our cleaning and ironing.

About two years ago I hired a lady to do my admin for me.

Then I got a gardener and last year a chap who comes around and cleans the cars.

Some friends were visiting recently and were getting quite worked up about how lazy AND extravagant we were having all these people to do things that we could easily do ourselves.

I explained that I actually saved money by being so reckless with my expenditures!

The total cost of all these people is about £1500 a month. But take the car cleaner, who costs me £50 a week, he saves me about 4 hours every week. Do you think that I can make more than £200 if I invest 16 hours of my time into new projects in my business? (If I can't then I should get a job cleaning cars) - ofcourse I can.

Overall much more of my time is available to invest into my business. This was the point that I made to my friends.

Sadly they were having none of it. They argued that if I wanted to I could work just as long and find the time to clean the cars/cut the lawn etc.

Whilst this is clearly nonsense unless I choose to rob time from somewhere else let's just assume that it is true for a moment.

How effective would I be if I was permanently running around trying to do all the little jobs that don't make me a penny as well as the big creative stuff?

 Not very is the answer. I focus on what brings in the cash and let other people do all the little bits that allow me to function. It also feels good not having to worry about that stuff which allows me to think more clearly and be more effective.

What about my wife who no longer works but still has the cleaner in? Yes, of course that's a bit extravagant but it makes her happy, and you can bet if she's happy then I'm happy!

26th March 2005

If you know your stats you will find it a lot easier to succeed.

Just recently a lot of people have been asking me how long a sales letter should be. The answer of course is as long as it needs to be to convince somebody to buy.

However that doesn't help much does it?

In truth people expect a sales letter to match the price of the item – cheap and cheerful needs only a short piece with few colours or snazzy bits.

Look at car brochures for example. Inexpensive cars warrant a thin brochure that is fairly factual, whereas a Bentley or high end Mercedes brochure uses thicker paper, much more posh photography, maybe a hardback cover and sells the lifestyle associated with the car, often by referencing it to other posh items.

Bentley, for example, talk about the clock being by Breitling and show pictures of rich folk at play. Mercedes suggest that you will do rather better at the golf club by parting with £100,000+ for a 2 seater convertible.

Both inevitably suggest that any man who owns one will also be accompanied by a stunning and sophisticated looking woman half his age! (No emails please, it's not my view at all) ;-)

Anyway, I was looking at the length of some of my successful letters and found that almost always my best selling products in the £50 - £100 range used about 4,500 words to sell them.

Whereas for more costly offers it usually took around 15,000 words to succeed.

When I reviewed all the copy in my "swipe file" of other people's letters I found that these numbers pretty much held true.

These facts are worth knowing on their own, but take a look at your own efforts and see how they compare; maybe it will show you how to improve your results.

14th May 2005

Is your price right?

Imagine wandering into a BMW dealership and seeing a line of shining cars all priced at what you think are "realistic" prices given their age, the model, engine size, extras fitted and apparent condition and then seeing one that is priced half or less than you imagine it would be.

Would you buy it quick or would you immediately ask yourself "I wonder what's wrong with that one"?

Similarly if you saw another shiny BMW at what appeared to be an inflated price you would probably say to yourself "I wonder what's better about that one?"

Most people assume that there is a reason for a price and a "proper" amount to charge. In reality prices are determined by what 'feels right' to the person setting the price and by what the market will pay.

Often the price that people expect to pay is more than we think.

I was recently involved in some price testing that showed conclusively that you can charge more for the same thing and sell more units, in fact when the price was doubled we sold twice as many units so we generated 4 times as much revenue.

This wasn't something for a few pennies either; the final price was nearly £2,000.

It always pays to try lots of prices, all higher than you think might work, just to see what happens!

24th June 2005

44

What sells best?

There is a famous story about the gold rush in the Klondike ... very few miners actually ever found gold but nevertheless some people got very rich indeed.

In fact the people who did best were those selling maps to "the gold fields" pickaxes and shovels ... In other words ... short cuts and tools.

People love to believe that they can get a short cut or advantage over everybody else and they love to buy tools to help them.

It's the same today, people buy diet books despite knowing that eating less and taking exercise is the ONLY way to lose weight. Some people love to buy racing tips and other "sure fire schemes" for making a killing without working.

However one of today's biggest markets is romantic shortcuts, in other words getting a date without all that fumbling around asking somebody out! (Fact is that I waited to be asked out by my wife, as she is now, 'cos I was too shy – groan).

There are all kinds of online dating agencies as well as speed dating and all manner of flirting websites - Try typing "how to flirt" into Google and see what I mean.

If you are thinking about your own business there is none better than one that sells short cuts and tools.

16th July 2005

Why self discipline is the one tool that you must have....

Self discipline is the one tool that you must have; probably think you have and most people lack.

You can get it but maybe not how you think.

Many times we hear people moaning about what they have or usually have not achieved, generally attributing their situation to "circumstances" or "lack of money/opportunity/ market/something or other".

I say that yes, in the short term, that may be the case but year after year can some people, most people in fact, really be so unlucky whilst a few others are always coming out on top?

Not really plausible is it?

There is only one mindset that successful people have and that is that they can AND will do whatever they set out to achieve.

No matter what they have to do, they make it happen.

Now so far I haven't said anything that you probably didn't secretly know or haven't heard before.

OK but knowing and doing are two different things.

You need just 3 things:

1) Know what you want, exactly. Do whatever is necessary to what you want. How much do you need to have in the bank/invested to retire/realise your dreams etc. This should be set in concrete.

2) Have a plan for getting there, worked out in exquisite detail. Know every twist and turn and when to take it, without this you might as well not bother. You don't expect to get anywhere nice if you just get in the car and take random turns do you? You might but there again you probably won't. However your plans should be set in sand - firm but able to take account of changes that happen on the way.

3) Most Important – Self Discipline. Lots of people do steps 1 & 2 but then do nothing. You have to become obsessed by your objectives. Two things to think about here – make working towards your goal a habit. I would not now dream of not starting work at 9:00am in the morning, I feel guilty if I don't. I may finish a few minutes later if I am going out but when I first worked for myself it seemed OK to wander in at lunchtime till I realised I would fail that way.

So I made a point of always starting the day as though I still had a job and soon got in the habit of clearing my day's tasks BEFORE going and having fun. When I still had a job I used to work on my business in the evenings again as soon as I got in (which I made sure was by a certain time – no stopping at the pub on my way home) and before eating.

The other thing to think about and it's a result of getting that good habit is that I will abandon ALL my other plans if my work is not done. No matter what fun I was planning I will give it up if I haven't got to where I wanted to be.

This forces me to focus on what I need to get done, in fact rather like when you have dinner guests and you can somehow hoover and tidy the whole house in half the usual time, because you have to, not going out and doing what you want until you have got to the point that you intended to makes sure that in fact you do succeed.

This self discipline applied to a well thought out plan will guarantee success.

14th August 2005

A willingness to stick with it and persevere is essential.

I am often asked by people if I will guarantee that they will make money, in fact only this week some madman was hectoring me on the telephone that "if I spend £70 on your DVDs I expect you to promise me that I will definitely make £5,000 a week...."

He didn't seem to think that he would play any part in his business just that cash would fall through his letterbox as a miraculous result of watching some telly!

I had to disappoint him and explain I was quite happy to provide him with the recipe and a list of ingredients, I would even answer his questions if he had any but it was his job to mix the ingredients together and "bake the cake".

He went off in a huff for some reason.

Now taking my recipe book analogy a stage further, quite obviously the first time Gordon Ramsay picked up an egg whisk he didn't have 3 Michelin Stars, I don't know but I imagine that he could even have bungled a simple recipe for cheese on toast his first time out. Obviously today things are a bit different.

I am quite certain that he doesn't get it right every time even now – he cooks every day I'm sure and still makes mistakes.

So it is with any worthwhile pursuit, your own business included. With perseverance and practise everybody improves but absolutely nobody is born already an expert in business (or cooking).

Many people I come across seem to give up at the first hurdle and are always looking for the easy way. In fact they often abandon promising enterprises because what appears an easier opportunity comes along. Don't get me wrong, I'm not saying that sometimes the ability to leapfrog ahead or gain some advantage won't present itself but I do think that some people will jump from one scheme to another (or one recipe book to another) if they don't get instant success.

Rock bottom if the recipe has been shown to work by other people and it appeals to you then stick with it until you've mastered it - in the long run it's quicker anyway.

10th September 2005

Get the best advice that you can possibly afford.

There are advantages to working for yourself, often in the field of saving tax which ultimately means that you have to earn less to enjoy the same standard of living as somebody in a job.

This week I had to file my 2004 accounts and was again surprised, as I always am, at how much the tax system is geared in favour of the small businessman.

For example there are ways of completely avoiding the crippling National Insurance charges that most people suffer (with little hope of getting anything worthwhile back).

Overall I have noticed that most wealthy people pay much less tax as a percentage of their earnings than the rest of the population, in fact in some cases they pay virtually nothing at all.

For example I was recently discussing tax saving schemes with a wealthy friend who mentioned that he had paid a firm of tax consultants £90,000 in fees. Whilst I was coughing and spluttering he went on to explain that this firm's scheme had saved him paying a penny of tax on his £1.7Million Pound earnings last year.

So if you take his overall situation he paid 5.3% of his earnings in tax advice but paid nothing more.

Of course this particular scheme was only appropriate to very high earning people and in fact has been stopped for next year (the government bring out new laws to try and gather more and more tax all the time whilst top tax specialists dream up legal ways of avoiding them).

However on a more down to earth level I have several friends who run little businesses where they earn £40,000 or £50,000 a year and quite legally pay little or no tax at all.

Compare this to the £20,000 or so in tax/NI that a good friend of mine pays on his £50,000 salary and you see why I say your own business has advantages.

So how is it done? Well not by getting advice from your mate at the pub or even from me but by ensuring that you employ a first class accountant who knows the rules and schemes that are applicable to your size of business.

It's no good getting a basic book keeper for a multi-million pound company but it's also useless trying to get an accountant who advises ICI to look after a corner shop.

My lady who does my accounts specialises in my size of business and I reckon she saves me about 20 times what I pay her.

So it really does pay, immediately to employ the very best that you can afford.

1st October 2005

Do you wash your car every Sunday?

During the week I had several lengthy discussions with a work colleague about his dwindling interest in his work.

On one occasion he threw his bits of paper down and declared that he was "not doing this anymore". As we talked about this little episode he told me that he was bored and could no longer be bothered with what he is paid to do and wants to do other "more exciting" things. Of course the thing he is now doing was the new exciting thing that he wanted to do a couple of years ago.

He admitted that despite being very talented he has never stuck at anything for more than a couple of years. I must admit to having some sympathy because I have often moved jobs (when I had one) every 2 years as well.

Fortunately I always managed to get promoted, however this chap is self destructive and has been fired or moved sideways and is heading the same way again. Like many such people he proclaims that he doesn't care, "I'll get a job stacking shelves" which is a bit of a waste for a man with a Ph.D.

The fact is that he is not thinking clearly and looking after himself. What he should be doing is planning for the future and investing his spare time and money in learning whatever he needs to know in order to improve himself and move on but instead he is just moaning and griping about his lot in life, claiming that he is too busy to do anything about his situation and not actually doing anything to change it.

OK point made but what does that have to do with washing the car?

Well my car is washed every weekend without fail, yes I admit I employ somebody to do it but in truth that has only happened this year – up until about a year ago I used to be out with the hosepipe myself. Similarly I have always had my cars, even when I drove old clunkers, meticulously serviced and repaired.

My chum? His car is filthy and as long as I have known him his cars have always been filthy. As for servicing he puts them into the garage for the minimum of repairs when he has no other choice.

I treat my car, like I approach life, as worth looking after – it will last longer, run better, reflect better on me and ultimately make me happier – after all who likes driving a dirty car that breaks down a lot?

Using your spare time to invest in yourself and making the most of what you have and can be makes a lot more sense that just griping and moaning!

9th Oct 2005

Focus is a key to success.

I am lazy. I know that I must be because my teachers told me so and I regularly have this personal failing confirmed by the ultimate authority on all things – my wife - otherwise known as "'She Who Must...'.

This unfortunate state of affairs has always led in the past to my taking on tasks that I am well able to do but never quite finishing them. One of the favourite dinner party anecdotes at 'Lowe Towers' concerns a roll of carpet that sat on the stairs for so long waiting to be carried up to the bathroom and fitted that she gave it a birthday card, a "third" birthday card in fact!

However, having managed to overcome my inherent inertia and make a bit of a success of my business I have been able to hire other people to take care of most tasks that I can't be bothered with.

Sadly though whenever I don't keep an eye on things the old idleness takes hold and I have bouts of doing nothing to move the business forward. The truth is that if I do nothing for months on end I can still live comfortably so I have to set myself goals of things that I want just to get myself moving.

This results in a sudden realisation that I have been slacking and a zeal to correct the situation.

In other words when I take a decision to set myself goals and do so, all of a sudden what I need to do in order to achieve those goals comes sharply into focus and so long as I keep my eye on that I can do in an hour what was taking me all week just the month before.

I have to force myself to set those goals but after that, everything is fine.

So the moral is force yourself to take the actions and you will be pleasantly surprised at the outcome!

15th October 2005

Upgrades mean bigger profits ... and why I paid £40 for a paper tablecloth.

This weekend I find myself in very unfamiliar territory.

My family convinced me that I would enjoy a weekend at Butlins in Minehead. Some band were playing here Saturday night so that apparently makes it worthwhile driving for 5 hours to get here only to stay in converted Army barracks euphemistically described as "Gold Standard".

However whilst I have been here, seeking any diversion from the enforced Bingo and knobbly knees competitions (at least I assume that these things still go on - I've tried to avoid actually finding out) I have been quietly impressed by some rather cute marketing that is quite blatant but still works extremely well.

Firstly it wasn't cheap, as I explained to 'She Who Must...' we could have stayed in a 5 Star Hotel for a lot Less ("Ah, but no band that way Timmy" - I've learned just to nod and groan quietly). Anyway she booked the only accommodation that was left which was termed "Silver".

Evidently there is a lower grade (Bronze perhaps?) and Gold and Deluxe. When we arrived at Silver check-in (Gold and Deluxe has a separate check-in closer to the entrance) it became clear that "due to cancellations" there were some spare Gold rooms and it was possible to upgrade. I was astonished to see many people, me included, paying an extra £180+ for the weekend for a better room, based entirely on the fact that the check-in was more exclusive – nobody had seen either room as far as I could tell. When we did, we found that we still were in converted barracks with metal camp beds but with an extra room with a couple of sofas and a bigger telly and had lost a bath in favour of a shower.

Most importantly, as it turned out, we also now were provided with towels, which is just as well as I would never have thought to bring my own.

One would have thought that this would have taught me a lesson but that same night at the canteen I was caught again. Lucky me was offered the chance to "upgrade" from the standard canteen to "The Yacht Club Restaurant".

Now here's the really clever part. Take one large building that was all used as a canteen. Put up a partition and lay cheap carpet in place of lino, use the same furniture and then stick paper tablecloths over them put exactly the same type of cheap, "motorway service station 10 years ago" fodder out on ever so slightly posher buffet carts and charge mugs like me an extra £40 to use this bit!

Remembering that I'd already paid for the food, and I had to eat it somewhere all I got that cost any extra money was a paper tablecloth on my table and by the way because you tell people to use the same table throughout their stay you needn't change this tablecloth because if it's dirty they only have themselves to blame.

The thing is that there will always be a ready supply of people who, even when they know they are getting poor value, will always go for the better and more expensive option, if only to feel more exclusive.

Try it, I promise that if you offer a deluxe version people will buy it, no matter how limited the extra features.

30th October

Why it pays big dividends to make allowances for the foibles of other people.

I have a short fuse. I am one of those people who growl the moment that something is not right but equally I forget about it very quickly.

Many times in my business I have snapped and snarled at people, often with good reason, sometimes without. By and large my outbursts have been overlooked and we have all carried on.

Occasionally somebody close to me has taken exception, and decided to end our relationship.

Just yesterday a friend wrote me what I felt was a really quite unreasonable email that made me want to get in the car and go and see him face to face for a "bit of a chat".

Instead I wrote a reply immediately (but didn't send it) reviewed it a few hours later once I was calm and toned it right down then sent it.

My chum replied pretty much straight back with a "sorry mate, having a bad day, didn't mean it how it came out" type of reply and now it's all behind us and we will continue to be good friends as well as making money by doing business with each other.

Conversely I have noticed that those people who cannot do this and would have to end the relationship tend to be failures.

They have a string of relationships, both personal and business that could have been great but that they have ended with the consequence that they are normally lonely and generally either struggling in some grotty job or with a business that never really prospers.

A worthwhile by-product of this "forgive and forget" approach is that you will probably live a lot longer as well. I know many people who suffer from things as mundane as high blood pressure through to extreme mental illness as a direct result of getting all gnarled up and stressed out constantly.

12th November 2005

Changes are afoot for 'Bruce the Cloth'

This weekend is my first wedding anniversary so this evening we are having a rather special dinner which has necessitated investment in a new suit (which with my new found slimmer figure looks rather dashing).

So, running late as I often do, last night I had to go to the home of "Bruce the Cloth" tailor to the fuller figured (I haven't lost that much weight) and provider of all clothing supplies to the House of Lowe in order to pick up this suit after a final bit of adjusting.

Inevitably Bruce and got chatting about his business which although it enjoys good custom of course could do more.

As the evening progressed (by now Bruce had pressed me into a glass or two of Rioja and some nibbles) we talked about how he could get more done by being ruthless with his time and only deal with things which make him money and leave everything else to other people.

The conversation turned to ideas for making his shop more inviting, having places for ladies to sit and drink coffee whilst their men folk are trying on clothes and similar strategies for improving trade without spending much money.

About this point "Mrs Bruce" arrived home and was cheered to hear this conversation as evidently she had been saying the same things for some years.

Poor old Bruce virtually held his hands in the air and cried "enough" as he said something like "You two are pushing at an open door, I agree with a lot of what you are saying and should do something about it". I couldn't resist reminding him of a similar conversation a year or two ago when the same or similar plans had been discussed.

The poor man (who gets these tips by the way) will probably hide next time my car pulls into his car park but I think the point is worth making.

How many things do YOU know about your business or situation that you have been meaning to do something about but have not yet got around to.

If Bruce's planned changes are going to make him, say, another £25,000 a year (if they're not then he needs some different changes that will) then procrastinating for 3 years has cost him £75,000 and what further investments and improvements could he have done with that £75,000?

Equally what have you got sitting there that you've been meaning to do but haven't got around to yet and how much has it cost you?

What does your bonus say about you?

Many people don't realise but the bonuses can often be the reason that people buy a particular product.

Realistically bonuses need to address people's concerns with the product they are buying and ideally help with the project being sold. This is an analogy that I have used quite successfully with a couple of people recently:

Imagine that you go into a garage to look at buying a 2 year old Range Rover. You are nearly ready to buy but then you think about the servicing costs and the costs of parts should it break down. Then the salesman says "and don't worry about servicing because I will throw in 3 years free servicing for you", you're still worried about breakdowns though, the guy then says "oh, I nearly forgot, if you're worried about the possibility of an expensive breakdown you can purchase an extended full manufacturer's warranty for £995." You immediately start to wonder whether to spend that £995 when the guy says "tell you what if you buy this car today I'll give you that £995 warranty for nothing".

Your major concerns have now gone, it's going to be easy for you to buy this and not worry about that other stuff for ages.

Be careful though because it's easy to give so many bonuses that the deal looks dodgy, imagine our salesman now says "oh by the way, as you're our tenth customer today I am also going to give you a free car wash every week and this box of emergency items, including a torch, towrope, warning triangle, first aid kit, bandages, wheel inflation machine and a teddy bear for the children. Now I also am delighted to enter you in our prize draw to win back 100 times the price of your car and a second prize of a weekend in Benidorm....." you would almost certainly be put off and think "I don't want that load of old rubbish, there must be something dodgy about this car if their giving me so much other stuff for nothing".

I hope this story lets you see why bonuses should be sensible, useful, relevant, appropriate and above all proportionate.

3rd December 2005

OK, so what ARE you going to do next year?

A few weeks ago I had my usual festive rant about planning for next year and knowing exactly what you are going to do to get where you want to be.

That was actually on the 5th November, 5 whole weeks ago and I know that almost nobody reading these tips has done anything about it.

People emailed me last time thanking me for the timely reminder and I bet they still haven't done anything concrete!

I got to wondering why that is. So much so, that I am launching a product in January to help people with this but I never promote stuff in these tips so I'll not say anything more about that here.

I found several reasons for this when I looked at it more closely and discussed it with real experts but one big issue was something I call "Countdown to Christmas". Basically most people are so wrapped up in getting ready for and looking forward to the biggest event of the year that they simply don't look beyond it.

In reality it is just another day but it symbolises so much, not in terms of religion, although that is obviously important to many people, but for all of its childhood associations and expectations. A lot of people see it as defining their year and cannot think past it.

Of course once that one magical day has been and gone those same people look glumly ahead to a whole year of toil stretching out ahead of them with little or no change from last year and only next Christmas to look forward to!

And then they start to think "if only I'd bothered to get my plans in place earlier". The fact that they haven't then debilitates them from further action.

What I am saying here is that it is never too late to change your life unless you want it to be. So if you haven't made your plans for next year, even if you do it now over Christmas, that is a lot better than never doing it at all.

12th December 2005

A Happy New Year...?

Life has downs as well as ups and you need to know how to handle them rather than relying on "knee jerk" reactions which may not get you where you want to be.

The last few weeks have been a bit troubled for me, although we've had a great holiday and a fantastic Christmas (and we're off for some sunshine in Madeira in the morning) there has been a niggling little voice nagging away at me for weeks now.

Basically what it is saying is that I have been robbed by a person who I thought of as a close friend; literally he has found a way to swindle thousands of pounds through the back door that simply does not belong to him, although in fairness it was a small percentage of my profits so it hasn't actually hurt me.

It would be easy for me to make this tip about keeping an eye on everybody and trusting nobody but I already did that and he still nearly got away with it. It is pretty well obvious that, if you're careful and vigilant, sooner or later you will learn of these crooks and stop their antics but I have a different point to make.

What do I do now? The trouble is that I like the man and, rather like the partner who forgives a cheating spouse, I am inclined to ask "why?" and "how could you do that?" rather than simply taking a baseball bat to his manhood (which my ordinarily placid wife feels would be more appropriate).

You always think you know what you would do until confronted by the reality at which point it all gets a bit more complicated.

I decided to think things through and make an informed choice about how I would handle this "friend" in the future once I'd given him a chance to come clean.

So for what it's worth (I hope this never happens to you) here's how I have handled it. Firstly I've changed things so that he can't get any more cash, then I've made it pretty clear to him that I know what's been going on without actually accusing anybody of anything or even talking about it. So I've put the ball in his court, if he comes to me and is man enough to admit his little scheme then I can decide if I can forgive and, over time, forget about it.

If he doesn't do that then he can obviously expect to lose my friendship but he can also expect, when he least expects it (if you see what I mean) a furious vengeance so complete that he will truly wish that he had never touched a penny.

Now you may think that a little extreme but I have learned that as George "Dubbya" Bush once said (and he doesn't often make sense but he did this day) "You are either with us or you are against us" and if you are against somebody you must expect them to put up a fight and sadly, in a fight, it's only winning that counts.

1st January 2006

Think it all through first.

Do you ever lay in bed at night, maybe for hours, just thinking about how you might do something, whether it is building a patio, starting a business or negotiating some deal?

I do – I tell you this at the risk of being seen as a complete fruitcake ('She Who Must...' will tell you that I am barking mad and past caring anyway!)

Imagine that I take it into my head to build a patio or some decking or a "water feature" in the garden. I will sit in the armchair or lay in bed for hours thinking through every single detail, every joint or border or cut that needs to be made. I will probably never commit any of this to paper but if I do it will only be after I know how the whole thing will look. The paper version would only be to calculate dimensions or show somebody else what I'm doing.

I am the sale before I take any action that may have a serious consequence later or that may need explanation. For example if I am involved in a long term deal with somebody I will try to think through every possible thing that may happen and anticipate what I would do, then I would think about how to phrase my intended actions should somebody ask me about it.

If I want to persuade somebody to my way of thinking I will consider every argument that they may use and carefully work out a counter to it that makes sense ... this process may take weeks but is, I think, time very well spent!

Not only do I nearly always get my point across but it's not often that something comes up that I haven't considered and already have a plan to deal with – of course it happens but then I have the time to deal with it because pretty much everything else is taken care of already.

4th January 2006

Get your point across, and sell more, by being different.

When I started writing these tips, as far as I know, I was the only person in the UK doing so. Now there are half a dozen or more people doing the same.

When I first wrote my ad that starts "Copy This Idea" it was unique, now every week I see at least 5 or 6, sometimes 10 or 12 ads with the same or similar headline.

It doesn't really affect me because I have so many different things going on but these people are not doing themselves and their fledging businesses any good at all.

Conversely I have a customer who has certainly copied my methods but has created a site that, whilst it is similar in function to my sites, is very different to look at. He also uses a completely novel ad and in fact, much to my chagrin, outsells me.

In fact his success reminded me to write some new ads as just lately I had allowed my sales to stagnate and now I have a new target to aim for!

Really, you will find that if you strive to do things a little differently to everybody else then you will get noticed and provided your message is clear and well presented you will undoubtedly sell a great deal more than just copying what everybody else is doing.   28th January 2006

Losing money can sometimes be the only way to make a profit....

Eh...?

It's expensive to find customers - although I make a good profit from my advertising in the national press I know many marketers using mail shots and internet marketing to acquire new customers who are grateful if they just "break-even".

It seems odd at first but what they are hoping is that some of those customers will buy something else, not necessarily today or even this year but at some point a profit will be made.

In fact many businesses now accept that they will lose money dealing with almost all of their customers and make their profits from a select few who either buy more or pay more for the same goods.

The easiest place to see this working is in hotel rooms and aeroplane flights. Everybody now accepts that you pay more for a flight if its nearly full when you book and common sense tells us that airlines can't make a profit selling seats for a couple of pounds on a multi-million pound machine that uses fuel by the tonne just to take off.

I know of one well known marketer who has worked out what his profits are on the fourth sale he makes and is prepared to break-even overall on the first three (actually losing money on the first two sales) in order to get the fourth highly profitable sale.

Sometimes, in very competitive markets this is the only way to survive. Of course the better alternative is to adopt novel marketing methods that gain you customers at a profit, which is why I continue to use my web-ads model!

18 February 2006

Be firm with Wallys...

Be prepared to be firm with Wallys, otherwise you'll spend all your time answering emails and taking phone calls.

One of the things that is most valuable to all of us is our time. I try (but don't always succeed) to guard mine jealously.

I have found that I am increasingly inundated with emails, many of the general spam variety but also a good number from customers and potential customers.

Frequently people ask the most absurd or intrusive questions and it is quite easy to be so annoyed by them that you can end up answering something which actually doesn't deserve your attention.

For example I have lost count of the number of people who want to come and meet me and have a tour of my office, home car and meet my family before parting with the price of a Curry. I used to accommodate these requests until the day that some lunatic kept me talking in my kitchen for 2 hours only to announce that he no longer felt the need to buy anything from me as I had told him all he wanted to know.

That wasn't so bad but he insisted on using the toilet before leaving and when he emerged he decided to try and have a quick sneaky look around my house. He got quite aggressive when I caught him. Never again!

Just lately people have started asking for copies of bank statements, frankly in these days of identity theft you'd have to be bonkers to send anybody who you didn't know well anything like that.

The trouble is that some people get nasty when you say no and then you can end up wasting time with a pointless exchange of emails.

My policy now is to try and answer all emails politely but if I sense a Wally at the other end then I explain that I don't have time to answer lots of questions and that my work always has a money back offer so take a look and send it back if you don't like it.

After that unless it's something sensible I just ignore, them. Sometimes it's really hard because some people try and provoke a reaction (I only know because some are so peculiar that they write and say this is what they are doing!) but I've had to do this when I realised that I was spending over 20 hours a week answering ridiculous enquiries.

I am not suggesting ignoring sensible and realistic questions from people who have bought or stand a good chance of buying but I am saying I have had to learn to give up quickly on nutters and time wasters. In other words rather than trying to please everybody, which obviously isn't possible I concentrate on looking after those people who are worth it!

5th March 2006

The silly little "secret" that brought me in an extra £140,000 in 7 weeks...

Not that long after I started in this type of business I acquired the rights to a product that was good but a little tired. Other people had sold many thousands of sets of this particular set of videos so I picked it up quite cheaply.

I also had access to some sales copy that went with it but again the trouble was that it had been sent to hundreds of thousands of people over a 2 year period.

I thought about how I might get new copy done and for a while tried to do just that, without a whole lot of luck!

Then I had a stroke of inspiration (my wife would say that somebody else gave me an idea, because I'm incapable of thinking for myself apparently – especially in regard to the location of my shirts!)

When you look at a website or read a sales letter have you noticed how you glance at the front and then, if you are a little interested, you turn it over (or scroll down) looking for the price?

It occurred to me that the vast majority of people don't read the middle bit.

So all I needed to do was catch the attention of the people who only glanced at the first page and give them something completely different to look at and a whole new world of customers would open up.

Just because people rejected the first letter doesn't mean that they will do the same second time around if it looks different, in fact even if it's the same they may still buy it, after all they may have intended to and then got distracted or may just be in a different mood.

Colours, layout, headlines, photos and many other things will all contribute to a "feeling" that will appeal to some people and not others – this is how two supermarkets can exist selling the same goods at the same prices side by side.

This technique (I'm told it's called "re-papering" by those who know about such things) is one of the cleverest tools in the box but is often overlooked, by me included, as it seems too simple.

How effective is it? Well on one memorable occasion I used this on a product that I had already sold over 6,000 sets of and was struggling to sell with the letter that I had. Honestly, I put in about 2 days work just fiddling around with it, changing colours, layouts and photos - seven weeks later I had sold over £140,000 worth of that product.

 It's not "rocket science" just a bit of simple logic thinking about what people actually do!

26th March 2006

The difference between a flop and a hit can all be in the....

The difference between a flop and a hit can all be in the description of the product. In fact if you are selling from a website what else does the customer have to go on?

They cannot actually see your product so they rely totally on what you say about it and any pictures you choose to use.

Obviously one of the things that tells them a lot about the item is its name.

Imagine that I am selling pencils with the following name: "Lowe's basic lead pencil", assuming a similar price and no other marketing I suspect that I would not sell as many as if I used the name: "Lowe's extra durable professional grade pencil".

They could easily be the same item but are perceived as completely different products.

About 4 years ago I had the rights to a product called "Product Development" which is hardly exciting, so instead we called it "How to Make £30,000 a Month Working from Home". It was the same thing but sounded a whole lot more enticing. The name came from the real results of what was revealed to buyers, which of course was all about developing your own products.

The thing is that very few people want to make products, what most people want to do is sell products to make a load of money, and if they can do that easily, that is without leaving their own home, then they like that even more, hence the name was much better anyway.

The name of something can often flow into the description as well. In the case above it was much better talking about the joys of working from home and those that had done so already rather than trying to explain what developing your own products was, all about.

You might of course be tempted to imagine that people really want to know what a product is all about before they buy it.

I don't think they do really, you don't think about what is in a sausage or the fact that it has to be cooked before you can eat it, you think about the end result, that is, how good it tastes. (Apologies if you don't like sausages but I'm sure you can see my point).

1st April 2006

Allowing twice the time gets the job done quicker!

Pardon ...? My wife often accuses me of talking in riddles but honestly this makes sense.

Very often people talk to me and tell me that they are going to achieve some magnificent feat in no time at all, I usually suggest taking their time but often they are insistent that they have set a goal and are going to "hit it".

Now in itself setting a goal with a deadline is a superb idea and one that I wholeheartedly endorse.

However both the goal and the timescales have to be "do-able".

A couple of weeks ago a couple of people asked for my advice on putting an ad together for a product they had yet to acquire.

They had no product and no website and no idea what to do about either but they insisted that I should help them write their ad. I tried to explain that this would not work but they were sure that they were going to get a certain product (that I wasn't sure even existed) so off we went on the basis that all would be well inside a few days.

I spoke to them this week and they had completely given up on that project because they had not got the product they wanted - they were well and truly despondent and muttering about "nothing ever works for them".

I'm currently on holiday in Cyprus and it was quite hot outside this particular day so I used the two hours or so that I was sat inside out of the sun to search for a product for them. No, I couldn't find exactly what they wanted but I did find something that was probably actually better and would make more money.

They were amazed. In reality they set themselves an unrealistic objective and so were bound to fail, which for most people is the end of another dream.

On a similar note whilst I'm away I asked my "technical chum" to do some bits and pieces on a new idea of mine, he was certain that he could start on Wednesday and it would all be done by Friday (he is very competent so I had every reason to believe him) but an unexpected snag meant that it is still not quite finished.

It will probably take twice as long as he thought!

Hence my view that if you allow twice as long as you first thought you shouldn't get into a situation where you are so despondent that you have a long "lull" whilst you rethink everything or worse still where you give up altogether.

7th April 2006

If you want people to buy from you put some sunshine in your business!

Having spent the last couple of weeks in glorious sunshine in Cyprus (but not too hot yet, which is even better) I noticed something quite interesting about the way people behave and got to thinking about how to make use of that in my websites.

I realised that in fact most successful businesses already do this but may not know it.

So what am I rambling about? Well we had two afternoons of rain amongst generally perfect blue skies. Two things happened, firstly pretty much all the people were much less happy when the sun wasn't shining and secondly some people quickly got over any grumpiness about it and did something else but quite a few sat around moaning and feeling like it was somebody's fault that it was cloudy or raining.

So people were happier when the sun was shining and as a result I noticed that they would spend more money because I assume, they felt more positive. Just simple things like the change in colours when the sun shone would make people say positive things and be more cheery and get their wallets out much more readily!

The key thing though is how without the sunshine a lot of people became quite negative. Now you could be forgiven for thinking that this is to do with holiday expectations but in fact it is to do with light. Human beings almost universally feel less comfortable in the middle of the night (originally to do with associations with danger I believe – hence the expression "our darkest hour") and equally it's very hard to be negative sat outside on a very sunny day.

So how can we use this? Well we obviously cannot make the sun shine but we can make our websites "feel" like the sun is shining with correct use of colour and sunny, positive language.

Have a surf around and look at the colour balance and contrast on people's websites, I am betting that you will feel much more like reading a site that is bright and cheerful with positive language and a "sunny feel" to it.

Little tricks can help here, try ensuring that photos are taken in sunny conditions; you can use blue sky backgrounds behind your pages and even use those sunburst circles that you get through a camera lens in your backgrounds.

A decent graphics programme like Photoshop or Paint Shop Pro will let you create backgrounds easily and change the hue of photos so that they appear sunny.

The goal is to make those grumpy bods feel cheerful and jolly when they come to your site, it may not make them buy from you but they are an awful lot more likely to than when they are miserable!

16th April 2006

How to get sales letters written for you in a few days for the price of a good night at the pub.

One of the questions that I get asked most often is "How do you get your sales letters written?" or "Who writes your letters?"

The answer is that I write the shorter stuff myself and get a copywriter to do the longer letters.

By the way if you are ever tempted to use a copywriter be careful here because I have found it best to always write the basics of the letter myself and THEN give it to a copywriter to turn into something magical.

I have tried just giving a copywriter some tapes or DVDs to watch and then to write a letter but it has never been a success, they don't have the same depth of knowledge or enthusiasm as the person who is going to make their living from that product...

So, how to get that letter written without hiring a copywriter...? (Who can charge anything from a few hundred to many thousands of pounds).

The solution is to try some of the software that does it for you. There are several good ones, Armand Morin does one and so does Marlon Sanders, in both cases you can find them easily by searching in Google for their names and 'copywriting software'.

Previously I would have said that this type of software would produce a very "iffy" result but quite a number of people that I know are now having success with this approach.

However, don't slavishly take the results of the software's efforts and just use it as it is but instead use it as a means of creating the right sort of structure and a workable draft. You will need to tone down some Americanisms and remove some of the "hypey" style but it will certainly give you something that will almost certainly be better than you could do on your own.

Better still it will allow you to get something done in a few days that could take months of waiting before a copywriter even starts to look at it!

22nd April 2006

Why you can say literally anything at all in a sales letter and get away with it.

I can already feel the wave of angry emails coming my way!

Hang on just a minute though and try and understand something really important about sales letters.

I would NEVER suggest that you say anything about your product offers which is not true. BUT, remember that your potential customer will be buying from you based entirely upon the description of your product offer, so they will never see it until AFTER they have bought it – so long as it's true you can say anything at all about your offer.

For example, you may have chosen to package a CD in a sickening shade of green that would stop people even picking it up if it was in a shop but you need not mention that fact at all in a sales letter.

All you need to do is highlight the positive benefits of your offer; you could even say that your product comes packaged in a special luminous container that allows customers to find it in the dark (if you must use a nasty glow in the dark shade of green!).

People often get quite worked up about this and go around in circles in the belief that you must say what the product's author or developer said about it or at least something similar.

Often you are best off coming from a completely different angle, for example, if you happen to acquire rights to a product that many other people are also selling then why not change the name (if you can) and write a new sales letter telling people what you see as it's advantages.

Even better, if you feel that it would be better with some additional features why not package two different items together that complement each other and make your own "set".

By doing this you can even get over any rules about not changing the product name by simply calling your new two-piece set something that you like, without actually changing the names of the individual parts.

29th April 2006

The dos and don'ts of Joint Venture marketing.

Last week I talked about Joint Ventures being a very good way of getting hold of other people's products to sell to your own existing customers.

A lot of people emailed me and asked for a bit more information on this subject:

There is of course a second way of doing Joint Ventures which is to market your own product to other people's customer lists and if you're really clever you can help people sell their own products to their own list in return for a share of the extra profits that you help them make!

So, if you have a good list of loyal customers you should approach (email is fine) people with good products that you think your list will buy. Write a persuasive but short email that explains what's in it for the person you're writing to and why it will sell. Do all you can to make it easy for them to do the deal i.e. you need to offer to do all the work!

I would strongly recommend that you offer them at least 50% of the profits as most people will assume that to be fair, but will be mildly insulted by a lesser offer.

I get offers of JVs every day with some idiot wanting me to let him sell my products and him give me 10% of the profit, frankly I don't even reply.

Similarly if you have a great product (that your proposed partner does not already have access to themselves) then email them with a suggestion to market it to their list and why this will work. Again 50/50 is the norm.

I would not try the idea of helping somebody to sell their own product to their own list until you have a lot of success and credibility to point to!

Normally it takes very little thinking on the part of the person you are suggesting a JV to realise that a proposal is good but often you will still not get an answer because it looks like it will take a lot of time to organise.

You can overcome some of this issue by demonstrating how much of the work is already done, include links to a sample website and sample sales letters to show you are serious and easy to deal with.

Lastly, since you need to build trust with your partner, unless it's just too stupid to contemplate, go with whatever money collecting and order processing suggestions your partner wants as this can often make or break the deal.

Sunday 14th May 2006

The view from the "Scout Hut".

This week I've had a few people ask me how to judge the quality of a product that they are thinking of promoting, especially if they know nothing about the subject area.

The answer is simple really.

Get to know the subject! And the first step would be to buy the intended product. Then compare it to others, see if anybody has reviewed it online (be careful here though as you can normally find a lot of idle whingers who moan about everything no matter how good it is).

I suppose that rock bottom something that is really good will "feel" right. It will have an air of quality and usefulness about it.

If you would be happy with it then the chances are that other people would be too.

What, you may ask does that have to do with "Scout Huts"?

Well a very good friend of mine always takes the Mickey out of my office, which he calls the "Scout Hut".

The fact is that this building is better built than most houses and a lot more economical too. It's got cavity walls and double glazed windows and although it has no heating whatsoever it's always at a comfortable temperature.

However it's a log cabin in my garden, a very stout log cabin (the walls are 9" thick) but still a log cabin so hence "Scout Hut".

Why is it relevant? Because I know nothing about building log cabins but the moment I saw this one I knew that it was "right" and so does everybody else who comes here, it just looks and feels like you would expect. So it is with any product, if it looks and feels good then it probably is.

Sunday 4th June 2006

Making quality decisions on where to spend your time and money.

Almost every day I am bombarded with the latest "systems" for making some huge sum in 3 weeks, 3 days or 3 hours and I'm pretty certain that if I am then you are too!

Now some of these things are realistic and some are plain daft, and some are cleverly worded to be true but misleading.

I'm certainly not going to comment on which are which, but I do employ a system of my own to evaluate what I am likely to get out of spending my time reading what the promoter has to say.

In fact you may be surprised to learn that I often study other people's offers and systems as sometimes there is something useful to be learnt either from the system itself of from the way that it's marketed.

I think that common sense dictates that if somebody is claiming that you can make a large sum of money in, say, 6 months then that is something that you may well have seen happen in many businesses in your own experience so you can probably assume that the first test has been passed but if the claim is less believable, take a silly example, that somebody has made a million pounds in 3 hours, then you need to ask yourself if this is possible.

Of course if the person concerned is Bill Gates then yes it is, but there lies the trick, Bill Gates has resources that you don't so you most likely won't get the same results as he does.

A common trick used is to talk of results that somebody got selling to their existing customers, but of course you may not have any existing customers!

However the real killer test for me is this. Is what I am considering buying into an enhancement to my existing direction or a diversion from it.

So many times people will leap at each opportunity offered them, and even if everything they go for is sound and workable they forget that they are already trying to make sense of the last 10 programmes that they bought.

Personally I have a core direction and I will snap up anything that helps me with that mission or speeds it up but I am very careful to only take on a limited number of other ideas at any one time as I know from experience that I can only do so much and I actually do nothing at all when I try to focus in more than two or three areas.

Sunday 11th June 2006

Investment in training is always money well spent.

Last weekend the world Internet Summit was going on at Wembley. I was invited along and turned up on Thursday along with everybody else, but I must admit that I didn't stay for every session.

In fact I had intended to watch most of the sessions but was somewhat incapacitated on Friday by a night of Thai food, red wine and long conversations about why people don't follow through on stuff!

I was so ill that I left my hotel, went home and stayed in bed, which is almost unknown for me.

Anyway, despite a two hour journey each way (mostly sat in traffic in London) I returned on Sunday and was extremely glad that I did.

I was able to watch an inspired presentation by a chap called John Childers who taught me many things about presenting to groups of people that I wished I'd known years ago.

I was so impressed that I invested in his $30,000 personal tuition (makes mine seem bargain basement I thought!)

I know that I learned things in his hour and a half talk that afternoon which will be worth much more to me than his fee and I got them for the price of a 4 hour car journey, which is not very much at all really; so I know that his full 3 or 4 day workshop is going to make me a small mountain of extra revenue this year and next!

In fact I got just as much from watching how he did things as I did from listening to what he was actually teaching.

I would recommend that no matter how much of a bore it may seem you read every business/development book that you have and watch every video and DVD on these subjects that you have bought because somewhere in them you will find real gems that will make all the difference to you.

I wouldn't mind betting that what I learned last Sunday could be the "spark" that helps me to double my income next year, and that's a big number to double!

Sunday 2nd July 2006

Don't be fooled by sunshine...

It is very easy when the sun is shining, as it has been for the last few weeks to ignore all of your goals and objectives for changing the way your life or business is and simply sit back and bask in the warmth. Life seems good when we can sit around eating and barbequing outside, with a cold beer or glass of wine and we forget how infrequently we can do this.

The sunny weather makes almost everybody mellow and relaxed (I say "almost everybody" because a friend of mine does nothing but whinge about the heat and longs for a bit of rain).

The trouble is that it doesn't last and on a day like today (at least where I am) as it pours with rain we suddenly realise that in two week's time most of the schools start the summer holidays. For some reason people always see this as a bad time to try and do anything (I even heard my wife, 'She Who Must...', saying something about "let's get the summer holidays out of the way first...". I thought she'd gone mad that's one eighth of the entire year that's being written off).

Anyway, we are over half way through the year and I would happily bet my new car on the fact that almost nobody reading this has made much progress on the things they were "going to do" this year, those "New Year's resolutions" are a bit dusty and forgotten in most cases.

I normally make the point about December time that people need to have their plans in place for the coming year.

I thought it also worth mentioning that if you're planning on slowing down whilst the kids are on holiday, come September you will have exactly 11 weeks until the time that everybody focuses completely on Christmas. Not long after you will be sitting at the start of another New Year making another "resolution" that will probably go the same way as all the others!

If you're going to change things - TODAY - whatever day that is, rain or shine, is the day to take action! Do something towards your goals every day, no matter how small, at least it is progress.

Surprise and delight with over-delivery.

Last night my wife - if you're 'newish' to my tips usually referred to by me as 'She Who Must...' – this is irony by the way as my wife is the sweetest, least demanding person I know (and she reads my tips!) anyway we took some friends out to dinner at a rather fine hotel just outside Winchester.

Obviously we didn't want to drink and drive and Winchester is a fair trek from home for us and our friends so a taxi was a non-starter so I got us a couple of rooms.

They turned out to be decent sized suites although I'd only asked for rooms. The hotel explained that they were having a promotion on these suites as they had just been totally renovated and they were keen for people to use them.

It was actually cheaper for the suite than the usual cost of a standard room so that in itself was generous, however when we got to our room I was again very pleasantly surprised as we had been given some fantastic toiletries, hand-made chocolates, flowers and a very good bottle of Champagne, all in the price!

When I thanked them they said that the special offer on the suite came with that so we ought to have it too.

The thing is that they didn't need to do this, I would never have known if we'd just been given a normal room at the normal price and equally I certainly had no expectation at all that we would get all the extra goodies.

The suite was fantastic but the bathroom was glorious, it didn't have a shower, it had a wet room which was big enough for probably 12 people (not that I shower with 12 other people!) and a Jacuzzi big enough for 2.

But that wasn't the most impressive thing.

The meal was an 8 course 'taster' where you have a little bit of lots of different things on the menu and each course had its own wine to go with it.

I was expecting measly little sips of the wine but the chap made it quite clear that we could have as much as we wanted (a dangerous thing with so many courses, I could have needed another day just to sober up!)

Other than making you wonder if you can fit such an occasion into your summer diet (http://www.timsminions.com/t always introduces a Summer diet regime around June/July, I've no idea why, I always ignore it) why am I banging on about this?

Simple. Do you think we'll go back? Do you think we'll recommend it to other people? Of course the answer is yes.

However it's not because it was good, I go to lots of good places. It's because it was BETTER than I expected, a lot better.

I try to do this with my own business, whenever I can I try to give people more than they were expecting. You cannot delight everybody (some people are grumpy no matter what you do) but by and large people tell me that they were pleasantly surprised by what they got, especially on the 'big ticket' items (obviously there is more money to spare for extras with higher price stuff).

If you can, try to surprise your customer with a little extra they weren't expecting, they are much more likely to buy from you again and recommend you to other people.

Sunday 16th July 2006

Why failure is good!

Or rather why what I like to call "testing" is the key to a fortune.

When I first started in this business my first project wasn't a great success, neither was my second or in fact my third.

Yes I had some success but not often enough or for long enough to rub my hands with glee and start dreaming of big houses and Rolex watches.

In order to get my web-ads working properly I tried a lot of different ads and a lot of website configurations.

Almost all of it worked to some extent but it took a lot of patient development to get to consistent big numbers.

For example my first really successful ad only worked in 3 different newspapers, I don't know why, it just didn't appeal to readers of the others.

I could have easily decided that the other newspapers "didn't work" but instead on my fourth project I tried them all again and found 7 that worked well.

Since then I have found sometimes a product appeals to a particular readership and sometimes it doesn't. I have no idea why but nor do I need to know. So long as I test each new product everywhere that I can think of it doesn't really matter why it does or doesn't work, what matters is finding out where it works.

Equally I'm always trying to improve my websites, of course it makes life easier if I have an idea of why things work or don't but ultimately all that matters is that I discover what works best.

So often people want me to tell them which newspapers to advertise in and they become disheartened when I tell them that I don't know and that they need to test and go with what works.

They see this as a waste of time and money whereas in fact it is a very wise investment. After all if I had concluded on the basis of my third project that the only 3 newspapers to advertise in were the ones that worked that time I would never have had all of the revenue that has since come from the other 4, which probably amounts to hundreds of thousands of pounds.

Sunday 23rd July 2006

Just because it isn't slick doesn't mean that it isn't right.

This week I was doing a workshop and a man took me aside and asked me how he could possibly be expected to sell "How to" information products that were essentially recordings from seminars run by people who were great authorities on their subjects.

Frankly I was confounded because to my mind what is important in a product is what it does. If I buy something the most important thing is that it functions like it should and only secondly should it look good and be impressive.

Now sometimes how an item looks is a major priority.

Presentation really is "everything" in the restaurant business because a major part of what we are paying for is how good the food looks because that makes us want to eat it, which is its purpose after all.

But a car that is dirty is no less able to work as a taxi than a clean one, although that would change for a limousine!

So it is with information products. Obviously some people are concerned with presentation but frankly if some Multi-Millionaire is explaining how he made his money does it matter whether he is wearing shorts and a tee shirt or a handmade £2,000 suit?

The fact is that on this occasion it is the information which is of key importance and not the way the man is dressed or for that matter whether he uses a flashy Power-Point show or some hand written acetate slides!

Equally, in my experience, if buy a DVD which is cut from the middle of a set covering an entire event and it is entirely relevant to what I wanted I really don't see why anybody would object to it if it wasn't specifically recorded alone on that subject. What matters is the content, not the presentation of that content and where it came from.

In fact I have often found that recordings taken at very expensive seminars with restricted attendance are highly sought after as they are usually a lot cheaper than going in person and have the feeling of being "insider information".

To my way of thinking if I'm really hungry what I need is food and if that happens to be fish and chips eaten straight out of the paper then that is every bit as good at sating the hunger as a Michelin starred gourmet feast.

Sunday 30th July 2006

In business, in fact in life generally, you get exactly what you expect to get.

Don't worry, I'm not going to give you some mealy mouthed psycho babble about overcoming limiting beliefs and "karma" - 'She Who Must...' (my long suffering) wife would be the first to put me up for adoption if I took to wearing sandals, sporting jumpers made of knitted yoghurt and took on board any woolly-headed theories!

Of course there is a proven link between writing down your specific goals and how likely you are to achieve them – conversely it's pretty obvious that if you have no particular goal in mind you will arrive where you aimed for – nowhere – but that is not the point I'm trying to make.

I am referring to something much more businesslike and easy to see and implement.

When we stand in a queue in the bakery and ask for a loaf of bread that we can see in front of us we have an absolute expectation that providing we hand over our money we will get that loaf of bread.

Nobody would expect to be told that it's not our turn for the bread or that we are not worthy of the bread. However there are still countries where that may well be the response and people would not have that absolute belief that they were entitled to the bread.

If you were told that in your local High Street you would probably think it was a joke and then maybe become indignant and finally you would walk off and go to another bread shop, still convinced that you were entitled to buy bread.

This is actually the right attitude to succeed in any endeavour. It may seem a bit arrogant but you need to believe you have an absolute right to whatever it is that you are seeking.

This is the simple attitude - an expectation that people will simply do whatever you ask them to do (providing you are polite and courteous) – that people often can spot but not understand in others who are very successful.

Most of us have stood and wondered how certain people always seem to get exactly what they want in circumstances that we feel that we wouldn't get the same treatment in.

In truth all that is happening is that those people simply expect to get whatever they ask for in just the same way as the rest of us would expect to get that loaf of bread.

Try it, you'll be amazed!

Sunday 8th August 2006

You should never be afraid to charge what your product is worth.

Last week we were staying at a 5 star hotel in Malta. I was lucky enough to be able to book the Penthouse Suite which was more than 6 times the size of the normal double rooms - it was an amazing 100 feet long and over 30 feet wide with a terrace the same size again – 3 bedrooms, 2 bathrooms, lounge area with seating for 8, dining room, entrance hall, two luggage storage rooms, study and a full kitchen (I'm not sure what the kitchen was for in a hotel with 24 hour room service and 7 restaurants!)

The thing is that when I called to book (back in March) I was able to get the Penthouse for about 4 times the price of a double room rather than the at least 6 times and probably more like 8 or 9 times that I would have expected (pro-rata per square foot plus something for the exclusivity).

By the time that we arrived all of the 5 star hotels on the island (11 or 12, I think) were completely full, I know because 'She Who Must...' had such a good time that she talked me into staying longer only to find that we couldn't stay on where we were and couldn't get a room anywhere else comparable.

During the stay I got chatting to one of the managers who was worrying how they were going to meet ever increasing guest expectations whilst the prices that they were charging were dropping. I couldn't understand the problem. He told me that this hotel had the biggest rooms on the island and a list of features that was overall better than all of other hotels. Of course other hotels had one particular feature that might be better (more food choices or a better gym or something like that but overall "my" one was the clear winner). So why worry?

He told me that people just "won't pay". I said something flippant like "put the prices UP and spend the extra money making the service even better - after all you're already full so where else is the money going to come from?" He told me that a high priced Management Consultancy had said the same thing (which made me feel rather clever :-)).

So why not do it? He told me that they were worried that people wouldn't book if they were more expensive than other hotels – I told him that people would book BECAUSE they were more expensive!

People will always assume that something is better if you charge more for it conversely they will assume that something cheaper is not as good. (It's obviously a good idea to invest the extra revenue in providing a product or service that IS better).

The trick is to keep trying higher prices until you find the natural "ceiling" where overall profits would suffer through lower sales - I promise that you will be surprised at how high this ceiling can be.

Sunday 20th August 2006

The sure-fire, never fails, easiest way in the world to get really great testimonials!

This week a customer of mine wrote to me asking how she could get testimonials for her product when she has never sold it to anybody.

When I thought about it I recalled that a lot of people have asked me that in the past.

Now firstly I have to say that I am not overly convinced that testimonials on their own make much difference to whether people buy your product or not – which is why I hardly ever use them.

Most people assume they are made up unless there is so much detail about the person giving the testimonial that every cynical Wally-brain ever born can phone them up and hound them about what they said - it happens, I once gave too much detail away and had my customers literally phoned up dozens of times by the same few idiots who accused them of all sorts of collusion and skulduggery!

And I absolutely hate the American copywriting habit of putting testimonial boxes in the middle of a sales letter, often several times – it's horrible, although I must admit to doing it once!

Anyway, if you're going to try and use some testimonials in some way (a separate sheet of them can work well) then how do you get them?

Have you noticed how any new book always seems to have loads of positive reviews on the back cover even though it's only been out a day or two?

They get those by sending advance copies to loads of interested people and asking them for opinions.

So what is to stop you sending copies of your product to people who might be willing to comment and asking for an opinion?

And what is to say that those people should not be family, friends, business acquaintances and generally anybody who you can ask to take a look?

You should NEVER make up testimonials but you can certainly seek them from people who you know and of course you don't have to use any that you don't like.

One other thing that you might like to do: If you have a list of points that you want to get across with your testimonials why not ask people to comment on your product and in particular give their opinion on the particular features that you want to highlight?

It's really simple but I know that loads of people struggle with this!

Sunday 27th August 2006

My Homer Simpson "Doh" moment...

This week I was watching Dragon's Den on BBC2, which I have done for several years pretty much since the programme started.

I case you've never seen it there are 5 multi-millionaires (Dragons) sat in a Den who are pitched by a procession of hopeful business people to invest in their mainly fledging, businesses.

About half way through the programme one Dragon had declared himself not interested in a particular "pitch" but the remaining 4 still seemed to want to know more. To be honest I didn't think much to the idea and could see why Dragon 1 (Who is only in his thirties and worth about a quarter of a billion!) had said no to it.

In the end a very unusual thing happened, two of the Dragons offered the chap the investment he needed and the other two put in a better offer. They ended up fighting to give this chap money and actually gave him a better deal than he had asked for.

Aside from the fact that I felt a bit of a Wally for not seeing the potential straightaway (which I did eventually) I suddenly realised that I watch this every week for entertainment and have never noticed before what a superb source of ideas it is – especially when you realise that 5 people worth between them over half a billion are sitting giving their opinion on each new idea.

Doh!!!

I suppose the moral is that good new ideas are put in front of us all the time but we often just don't see them, especially if they are on the television which can somehow feel different to "our" world. The trick is not to overlook anything, no matter where we see it.

Sunday 17th September 2006

How to boost your chances of success in any and every new project that you start.

I've been back in our grey and wet country for only 12 days but I have already started to forget how much fun it was to be away and how pleasant it was to be almost certain that it would be warm enough to eat breakfast outside in the sunshine.

That got me thinking that Christmas was less than a month ago but most of us have already forgotten all about it, except I'm sure that the banks and card companies will be sending us a reminder of how much we spent any day now!

I was also wondering how many people are still sticking to their New Year's resolutions.

At the risk of misquoting some famous person (I've forgotten who it was) - the trouble is that "Life is what happens whilst your busy making other plans". We all do it, we all get sidetracked and distracted, some people are so lazy, and this is often me, they never even start to do the things they intended, let alone finish them.

But one thing I have noticed is that it is easy to do things that are habit, for example, I find it easy(ish) to get up at and start doing things early every weekday morning but at the weekends I just seem to find it easy to lay around reading a book - which would make me feel really guilty on a weekday. This is because I have habits which I acquired by repeatedly doing the same thing.

I was chatting to Andrew Reynolds about this the other day and he was telling me that he has recently been forcing himself to spend an hour a day on his business education, he is determined to make it a habit to do so (apparently you only need to do the same thing daily for a few weeks to create a new habit).

Now you could be forgiven for thinking that people like Andrew don't need to learn anything else about business, they already know enough surely? Now I know it's clichéd but none of us can ever afford to stop learning and I think that one of the big differences between people who move forward and those that fall by the wayside is this habit of continually learning.

Of course there are lots of other success habits as well but a good start is to force yourself to put time aside every day to learn new things - not what happened in Eastenders but something useful - and pretty soon that will be a habit. Then the stuff that you are learning everyday will soon start to pay dividends in your chosen business. You will also have shown yourself that you can stick to your plans and that will bring you huge rewards in how confident you feel about other things you plan to do.

Sunday 20th January 2008

Often the only way to get things done is to put yourself in a position where you have to do them...

I am extraordinarily idle, as my wife tells me endlessly, and I would probably agree.

I will put off doing things that I don't fancy for months or even years. Whilst I'm putting them off I find that they grow in my mind into seemingly insurmountable tasks.

Many years ago I put off doing my VAT return for over a year (you're supposed to do it every 3 months) the nice people at the VAT office were so fed up with me that they started sending unpleasant threatening letters so I had to buckle down and tackle a task that I was really loathing the very thought of starting.

I left it until the last possible moment and ended up doing it over Christmas - by now I thought it would take a week or more. It was actually easy, took me less than a day and I felt great to have got it out of the way.

I'm still the same now with all sorts of things but I have learned to force myself to get things done.

For example, say I have in mind a project that needs a mail shot doing and I don't fancy organising the sales copy. What I will do is tackle the easy parts first that will commit me to continuing.

So I will pick a date and buy stamps and envelopes. Then I will book the printing and people to put the printing in the envelopes so now I am in a situation where I have to do the bits I don't feel like doing otherwise I will lose most of the money that I have invested.

The prospect of losing money that has been spent seems to be a bigger motivator than the prospect of earning "new" money (I wouldn't put much effort into a scheme that promised me that I could make £50 but if I dropped a £50 note down a crack in the floorboards I would spend ages trying to fish it out!)

So I often deliberately go out on a financial limb to ensure that I follow through on my plans, if I don't do that I know that I will just let all manner of things drift and possibly never tackle them.

I'm not suggesting being silly here with money that you don't have but I am advocating ensuring your own success by making it really painful for yourself if you don't bother taking action. And of course the other side is that you will feel great when you have got things done that you were apprehensive about starting!

Sunday 27th January 2008

Think Big and Kick Ass...

No I haven't been dreaming about the Burger King menu again and wondering how much bigger my rear end might become!

This week, in line with what I was saying a few weeks ago about continuing to invest time and money in business education and always learning new ideas I've been reading a book by Donald Trump called "Think Big and Kick Ass in Business and in Life".

In case you don't know, Donald Trump is famous for, amongst other things, having an extremely dodgy comb over (called "a Donald" because it is so distinctive), being a Billionaire many times over, despite having nearly lost everything in the early 1990s and for doing the original "Apprentice" TV programme in the US before Sir Alan Sugar did it here.

Trump is quite remarkable in having started with very little but early in his career, after 18 months of effort, acquiring a sixty two million dollar option on a sizeable chunk of Manhattan without putting anything down at all. He has done all manner of very big and very astute deals since, usually in the face of many doomsayers telling him not to.

He later bought No.40 Wall Street for one million, against advice and promptly got some kind of tax break worth four million.

His book teaches many things, but one thread that runs through it is the principle that "seeing as you are thinking anyway, you might as well think big!"

He points out that many people just limit themselves by thinking too small and that those that set huge goals usually get huge rewards.

Put another way, if I tell myself that I am happy to accept, say, 1000 orders for some product, when I get to that point I am now happy and stop really trying to do anymore, even though there might be many more potential customers available.

Whereas, if I set my sights on 100,000 orders, I may not get to that point BUT I am going to be going after every last one and certainly way past the point that I would have stopped at before. Maybe I will miss my big goal and only get to 30,000 but that is still 30 times more than previously.

This kind of thinking is something that many of us have heard about BUT it is really easy to forget it when you are stuck in some dull job or pinned to the desk with day to day admin.

Donald's book is not particularly stylish or well written (like I can talk!) but well worth reading and implementing (there's loads of other good stuff).

So I guess there is another little tip there in not worrying about how good you are at something but just getting on and doing it anyway. When you do, set aside the time to plan, but don't dither and really think BIG, bigger than you are comfortable with, I think you will be surprised by the results.

How to avoid getting left behind with the dinosaurs and cooking the perfect Sunday Roast...

This week I was trying to explain a concept to a colleague of mine and remembered an old story which perfectly sums up what can easily happen to stymie progress in your business or life generally.

The story as I was told it goes that a newly married man sees his wife trimming off the last few inches of a large joint of meat before she puts it in a baking tray for their Sunday lunch.

Never having seen meat prepared this way he assumes that it is something to do with ensuring the meat is extra tasty so says nothing, however after a few weeks of seeing this he asks why his wife does it.

She explains that this is how her mother taught her to roast the meat, she doesn't know what the secret is but there is a good reason for it!

A few weeks later the couple are eating with the wife's parents and he asks his mother-in-law why she cuts the end off the meat before putting it in the roasting tin. She tells him that she doesn't know but that she remembers seeing her mother do it.

So a few weeks later he gets the chance to ask his wife's Grandmother why she cuts the end off the meat, is this in fact the secret to a great roast?

Her reply is simple, her husband always used to bring home a piece of meat that was far too big for the roasting dish so she always had to cut the end off to fit in the oven!

So here's the thing, so often we do things just because we always have or worse, because other people always have. We don't stop to think about why we do things and ask ourselves if this is the best way. Often it used to be the best way but things have changed and we have never reviewed what we are doing.

Recently I've been planning some training that I am going to be doing and have been surprised by how much has changed in my business in the last few years. There hasn't been one big shift in what I do but I've noticed that simple things like, for example, how we use stamps or don't use stamps has completely changed and our use of colour printing is now totally different to even a year ago.

My advice is to question everything that you do and ask if this is the best way in the current circumstances and with the technology available. If you don't know then test different approaches and see if what you are doing is still the best approach. This is equally right for a clothes shop as it is for an online business like mine.

And never be tempted NOT to do things just because nobody else does or because somebody who has no experience but big opinions tells you that you shouldn't!

Winners do what it takes...

It is Saturday afternoon and I am busy preparing for an overseas project that I'm involved in (I think I mentioned this last week), I have just called 'She Who Must...' and explained that I will not be in before midnight.

Bless her, all she said was "fine darling, are you eating out, shall I leave some food out for you or shall I wait up and cook when you get in?" I guess I am really lucky that she is so tolerant and understanding since I know many people whose wives would have a hissy fit if their husbands were not doing what was originally planned...and some men who are the same way with their wives.

To be frank, it has always been this way between us, I am hopelessly disorganised and she just works around my appalling time-keeping and habit of doing everything at the last minute. Often she has to reorder everything because of me and she hardly ever complains.

This unfailing support is, I'm sure, an important aspect of why I manage to make my business work.

However, it also highlights another important point.

Because I needed to get something done by a deadline I was beavering away on a Saturday night when other people were watching the TV, going out to dinner or down the pub. Yes I would have much preferred to be quaffing a big glass of red wine (an activity that I am enjoying more and more!) but I had work to do and that must come first if I want to carry on growing my business and enjoying the rewards.

Similarly, my good friend Andrew Reynolds sent me an email this morning which showed that he was up and about at 4:00am. He is hugely excited about his latest project and was busy putting the details together. Yes, he can afford to lay in bed for as long as he wants without ever needing to do another day's work but like almost all really successful business people he loves the thrill of launching new projects and getting involved in building businesses out of his latest ideas.

Neither of us is a workaholic, we both love to spend time relaxing and enjoy having a good laugh when we go out but when there is a job to be done the only thing to do is get on with it until it's finished, ignoring any distractions or whingeing from anybody who doesn't like it - in other words "do whatever it takes".

Honestly, I am chronically lazy, but the rewards of persistence really are worth it!

Sunday 17th February 2008

The money is in the detail...how's your helicopter view?

Many people tell me that details are just that and as such unimportant, "Tim you have to see the bigger picture".

I agree, seeing the big picture is really important BUT there is no doubt in my mind that the success of any project is definitely in the details.

Actually what you need, I think, is a helicopter view...you need to be able to hover above things and see the whole picture and then swoop down and focus on one tiny part, deal with it and then swoop off to the next thing that demands your attention.

Obviously that is simple enough but what are you looking for in those blessed details that I keep on about?

That is also simple - a perfect presentation of whatever idea you are trying to get across!

If I want to create an impression with a photograph I will happily spend hours getting one shot that says what I want it to say (with a digital camera you can take hundreds of shots and choose the best ones easily). Actually there is another really critical issue here, people like real photos of real people - professionally posed models are great for some things but let's say I'm trying to sell outsize men's clothes, it is no good having some gorgeous super fit looking model looking wonderful, people cannot relate to it, you need to use photos of the sort of people who will buy the product, in this example blokes who have visited the pie shop a bit too often! (But obviously looking their best in these great new clothes.)

With colours on brochures and websites I will often spend days thinking about what layout and colours will create just the look that I am after.

Equally obviously when things have to be written, again, a change of a few words can create a totally different meaning.

None of this is that complex or difficult to do but it does need a bit of thought, I learned a lot from just trying different things to see if my hunches were right but that can be expensive!

Another way is to get a group of interested people round a table and compare what each of you thinks is the right approach to a particular detail - you will be surprised that there is normally a consensus on what is the "right" picture or colour or wording etc.

You can learn a huge amount this way without any risk at all if you get it wrong.

Sunday 24th February 2008

10 years gone in a blink and time is speeding up...

When I sat down to write this tip and noticed the date, above, I decided to completely change what I was going to say - I'll save my story about the secret formula for doubling sales revenue I learned from a bottle of red wine for another week!

It is now March, a third of this year has nearly gone already.

I have been amazed since I started my first business in 1998 and then my current business in 2001, just how quickly the years have gone.

I know I am beginning to sound like all old people but as you reach your middle thirties (or early forties in my case) the years just "fly by" and honestly time seems to speed up.

I came back from celebrating the New Year in Dubai 2 months ago BUT it FEELS like about 2 weeks.

It will be Easter in 3 weeks and then it will be time for your summer holiday and we'll all be another year older - in fact I'm so worried now I think I might go back to my red wine story and try and forget how quickly my life is passing...

What's my point?

Well last night I was at a "boy's night out" (curry and indoor motor racing) talking to a friend who is 46 and planning a big world cruise and to buy a flashy sports car when he is 60. He can probably afford at least one of those things this year but he says he is too busy now and will do it when he retires.

I pointed out that he may not live to 60 (morbid but true, we just don't know what is around the corner) and if he had things he wanted to do then why wait to do them if he could do them now? He did not have an answer!

Most people simply put off doing things that they actually want to do but get on and do those things that they feel they ought to do. So yes, they get around to doing little things like their tax return (because they get told off if they don't) but they never get around to the bigger ones, that they would love to do, like starting their own business, because they don't have to. In fact I very nearly didn't start mine for that very reason.

I sat for years thinking about it and talking about it but never doing it, meanwhile I made my employers very rich in return for a relatively tiny salary (I never earned more than 8% of the profits I made for the company I worked for - now I get 100%).

So my message is simple, if you are going to start your own business do it now, today, this minute, OR, if not, then decide that you have no longer any interest in doing so and stop kidding yourself and wasting your time.

You're either going to do it or you're not but if you delude yourself that you are going to do something when you know really that you won't ever bother to start then all that happens is you regret your own lack of progress for ever more. You would feel much happier and better about yourself if you just got on with it, or decided, properly, that you were quitting and instead would make the best of your job until you retire.

Harsh words maybe, but we all need prodding occasionally! I have to thank my wife, "'She Who Must...'" for telling me almost exactly what I have just told you, 10 years ago and for the ensuing years that have been the most enjoyable of my entire life!

Since I am now in danger of becoming soft and soggy I wish you the best of luck!

Sunday 2nd March 2008

Never underestimate the value of just a handful of customers.

It's very easy when you start out to become despondent when you only have 2 or 3 orders a day coming in and you are barely covering your advertising costs BUT I worked out recently that 1000 customers (3 a day for a year) was worth about £300,000 to me in the first year or so and maybe as much as 3 times that over the next few years.

Far too many people lose sight of the fact that many customers buy from you more than once, in fact in some cases I have people who have made more than 8 fairly major purchases in 4 or 5 years and I know of other people in the business with customers buying products several times a year, for lots of years!

So long as what you are offering is something that people want and your service is good they will keep coming back for more. Whilst it is obviously true that you cannot make offers that appeal to everybody all of the time you can certainly appeal to a lot of people a lot of the time - and make a great living doing so.

Last Monday I flew to Scotland (on business), came home Tuesday night and on Good Friday flew to Cyprus where I am now on holiday.

Many people still have trouble believing it but the time really has arrived when you can work anywhere on a laptop and you don't need to be a big time corporate type or spend a fortune doing it.

Back at home I have a normal computer and broadband connection. I back this up onto CD and an external hard-drive every so often because this is my whole business. I have a laptop which I am writing to you on now; it is an everyday model costing a few hundred pounds.

Just in case you are wondering, I believe that it has been snowing and is a bit wet and windy back at home but here I really am currently enjoying the sunset sat on my balcony with a cocktail and bowl of pre-dinner nibbles. The view through some palm trees is truly stunning as is the sound of the waves gently breaking on a powder soft white sandy beach!

Sorry, when my sister called and told me it was snowing at home I couldn't resist a little tease!

Anyway, here I am connected by wireless on Sunday evening to the outside world...if I want to get anything off my computer at home I can log onto it remotely using a free service called www.logmein.com...in other words there is literally no difference between being at home and being in Scotland, or here in Cyprus or indeed in Australia...and it is not as though I have had to invest anything to get to this stage. Logmein is free, everywhere has wireless on demand now, often free, and computers are available everywhere at reasonable prices.

Yes I do get somebody to pop in and see if there is any post and yes I do use other people to send out the orders we get every day but again that is all available easily and cheaply. Should I have a technical problem, as I did yesterday, there is a service I use that sorts it out remotely as well for a few pounds!

I can truly be anywhere and be just as productive as if I was sat at home, probably more so because I am not bothered by everyday distractions.

You may just have one nagging thought...why is Tim working on holiday?

That's easy! I spend a huge amount of time abroad now, I am not tied by needing to be in the office so can work when I feel like it from wherever I happen to be. No I would not normally "feel like it" on a Sunday evening but I like to write these tips properly, as they occur to me, I don't have them saved up in advance ready to send out and this just seemed about the best advert for actually "getting on with it" that I could think of!

I'm going to spend the rest of the week scuba diving, loafing by the pool, reading a couple of books and, er...enjoying the local food and wine!

Sunday 23rd March 2008

Where to get brilliant products to sell with no competition...

This is probably the question I get asked more than any other.

The answer is that unless you either have a virtually unlimited budget and can therefore afford to buy worldwide EXCLUSIVE rights to somebody else's product or have the skills to develop and produce your own products then you have to have a few clever techniques at your disposal.

Quite simply, thinking of this as preparing a meal, you need to start off with decent raw ingredients that are affordable, so maybe a set of products that, say, 50 people will share between them. It doesn't really matter how many so long as it isn't thousands of people!

The trick here is to make sure you are buying from a reliable source, not some faceless website with somebody that you've never heard of selling "resale rights" for a few pounds. As in most things, you usually get what you pay for.

Then you need the recipe. This is the clever part because what you need to do is take what you have as raw ingredients and make something fresh and new.

So many people don't "get" this part and it is something that I always spend a lot of time on when I teach people face to face.

In the same way as if I take some eggs, cheese, tomatoes, mushrooms, bacon and bread, I can fry everything and make a nice fried breakfast (maybe leaving out the cheese), but can also discard some ingredients and make scrambled eggs on toast. Or I can make a range of different omelettes, loads of different sandwiches, which I could toast if I wanted, or I can get really creative and make things like the dish I had in Russia which was a small pot they called "mushroom pot". It was mushrooms baked in cheese and eggs and was fantastic (excuse me getting carried away, I am dieting this week!).

Hopefully you see the point, starting with the same raw ingredients you could make a myriad of different dishes which would appeal to different people. My dad would love the fried breakfast but never eat anything as fancy as the mushroom pot!

This way, only you have your particular mushroom pot, or omelettes or whatever and so you have just eliminated any competition and also made different things to appeal to different customers so you will make more overall sales.

There are a whole load of other clever little twists on this, like the equivalent of spicing the whole thing up, for just a few pence, with just a pinch of another ingredient, say chilli for example, but sadly I haven't got time or space to explain them all here!

I hope this makes sense!

Sunday 20th April 2008

Are money back guarantees worth the paper they're written on?

It's a funny thing but almost nobody has ever told me of a time when they sent something back for a refund and didn't get it.

Of course I have often listened to tales of woe from people who say that they got ripped off but almost invariably what has happened is that they either asked too late or sent something back that they had damaged so it couldn't be resold.

If a company offers a money back guarantee if you return your book or whatever in 30 days and you send it back after 40 you can hardly expect a refund but, oddly, some people do!

My personal take on this is if the item is of low cost, like a couple of DVDs, then I have little to lose by refunding somebody who is a bit late asking – that said, some complete idiot sent some old videos back after having them for 4 years with a note saying his video player has broken so these are no longer any use so he wanted a refund; I felt justified in saying no on that occasion!

Of course, if you are selling a high value item you do have to be careful as the temptation to copy, say, a £900 course, is very tempting for almost everybody.

In those cases I often suggest a half way house, for example you can offer to send your customer some of the course to see if they like it and feel it is worthwhile, if they send it back then they get all their money back but if they keep it then you send them the rest but once they have it all they cannot then get a refund. Computer Software is often sold a bit like this with a "lite" or trial version until you pay your money for the full version.

So long as you read the wording carefully and stick to the terms offered, at least in my experience, people are always pretty decent about refunds.

It is worth remembering that in many cases the customer is not actually entitled to a refund in law but the supplier has offered it as an incentive to get the customer to try something out so it is almost certain they will honour it because not to do so would damage a relationship they are obviously trying to build.

In the world of direct and internet marketing those relationships are often very long term with customers coming back and buying many times so it is not worth spoiling a relationship by not sticking to the deal (be aware though that nobody likes people who break deals and this works both ways and that customers who demand refunds they are not entitled to are perhaps not people anybody will want to deal with in the future).

If you look at this logically, it actually makes complete sense to take up any offer that you are even half tempted by if it has a sensible money back offer since you don't have to decide until you have seen, at least most of, the product or service.

I sometimes shake my head in despair at people who hem and haw about whether to attend a workshop or not, as they feel it is a lot of money if they don't like it.

Of course that is true and of course I believe that my workshops (and one or two other people's) are brilliant so what's not to like :-) but, seriously, it doesn't actually matter if you can sit and listen to me for most of the day and still get your money back if you don't like what I say!

Similarly, if you are starting out in this business, my advice is always to honour your guarantees, even if the customer really annoys you, if they are within the terms of the deal just give them their money back, it is much better for long term business!

Sunday 27th April 2008

Your product doesn't matter, price and copy is everything...

Firstly, my apologies for my lack of tip last week, I was presenting a workshop all weekend and fell behind with my other duties!

Just recently the same issue has come up time and again. People have been asking my opinion on whether their product (for selling online) will sell or not. They send me the product (no more please, my cupboard is full) and ask if it will sell.

Other than the first, somewhat sarcastic, answer that pops into my head (How do I know, I'm not clairvoyant, why don't you try and sell it and find out!) my real answer is: I don't know because you haven't told me anything about it, I need to know what you are going to say about it.

The crucial point that so many people forget is that nobody can see the product until AFTER they have bought it and it has been delivered.

The ONLY thing your customer has to go on is your sales letter and the price you are asking - if the copy is fantastic it will sell, regardless of how good or bad the actual product is (of course if it is bad you will get loads of them back!).

If your website is super smart, helps tell the story and keeps the customer interested and reading the copy then you will sell more, but poor copy on a beautiful website still won't sell.

Price needs to match the customer's expectations having read the copy.

When my wife (who knows everything that there is to know about shopping and spending money) goes shopping for a new handbag, she, like all of us, will make a judgement on how good something is based on its price. If, just for example, she sees a Versace handbag which she believes is normally £800 on sale for £25 she will consider it fake, even if it is not (Hopefully she won't buy it either way!!!)

Similarly, some bag on a market stall for £100 will just not get her to buy even though she might like it and would happily spend that amount because she will doubt its quality and believe it overpriced because it is a market stall.

Everything has to "add up" and "feel right", the price on a website needs to match the idea in our heads of what something is worth based on the copy and how everything else looks, too cheap is just as bad as too dear, in fact often worse. People will aspire to pay top dollar if they can but will immediately dismiss something cheap as being not good enough for what they need.

So if I am in doubt I always start my price testing high and come down if I have to, I have been frequently surprised at what people will pay!

Sunday 18th May 2008

How my tailor keeps his customers and gets away with his horrid old counter...

My tailor's name is Bruce (usually referred to as Bruce the cloth although he does carpets as well so I suppose Bruce the yarn would be better), so firstly I've got to apologise to him for calling his counter horrible.

But it is pretty nasty and so is his "sale bin" which is, I am certain, home made from bits of hardboard and left over lumps of wood from a shelving project.

The thing is that these less than ideal fittings are a bit off putting at first BUT, as far as I know, Bruce hardly ever loses a customer - certainly I would never dream of going anywhere else for clothes or carpets – because Bruce is such a great retailer in other ways.

The fact is that no one business can ever appeal to or please everybody, you just have to accept that some people will not like what you do. For example, I am somewhat stout and don't like venturing into shops that stop at a 44" chest, proclaiming that to be extra, extra large (What nonsense, these fashion fascists have clearly never seen a real man and his dinner plate!) so I am never going to go shopping somewhere that appears to cater to scrawny and undersized people.

Even shoe shops discriminate! I have size 13 feet, let's be honest I'm big in all directions but lots of thin people have big feet, however shop assistants in many high street shoe shops look at your with pity as though you have plague or some other soon to be terminal complaint when you ask for anything bigger than 11 or 12. Again, instead, I wander off to proper shops that sell shoes in all sizes up to gigantic.

However there are many, many people who would never go where I go, for a variety of their own reasons and that is fine.

So why do I always go to Bruce first? Simple, his overall package appeals to me. His service is great, he will go to extraordinary lengths to get any of his customers just what they want – many times I have gone in, liked a suit or shirt but found that, despite a huge stock, he either doesn't have my exact size or the colour I want.

Sometimes it's something small - I like double cuffs on shirts and he may only have a shirt I love with a single cuff but he has been willing to order just a shirt from Germany or France of some other exotic location and if need be have things altered when they get here all within my usually very short deadlines (have a habit of wanting it in 3 days time).

He doesn't even object if I don't like it when it turns up. He'll happily find me unusual clothes if I express some desire for a suit in an odd colour or a shirt that I once saw somebody else wearing.

Now, most people would imagine this shop would be expensive, but not a bit of it. Last year I noticed that he was selling silk ties for £20 that I would have thought would be £45 anywhere else. And when it comes time to pay, he always enjoys (well I enjoy anyway) a good haggle.

I'm so comfortable dealing with Bruce that we have chosen carpets, not asked the price, had them fitted and been PLEASANTLY surprised when the bill has arrived.

And does he treat all his customers as well as this? - Absolutely yes.

He will deliver if asked, has come round personally on a Sunday morning with alterations so I can catch a flight and will do just about anything a customer wants.

However, sometimes when you go in his shop, there is a queue and you have to wait. 45 minutes is not unusual as he runs around looking after everybody and being unfailingly pleasant. Sometimes you get a cup of coffee, it will be in an old mug but somehow that is fine. Sometimes you will get an alteration done whilst drinking that coffee or trying on something else. Not once has he ever pressured me into buying anything but I always leave with much more than I went in for.

For years I have ribbed him about the tatty parts and to his credit he has gradually been smartening up the shop fittings (he put in air-conditioning a year or two ago which is great because there is little worse than trying on clothes when you are hot and sticky).

But really it is everything taken together which makes it work so well, some people would hate it, but for me and his other loyal customers, you could put Bruce in a shed lit by candles and I would still go there for all my clothes.

So my message is this, accept that some people won't like what you do and play to your strengths, accentuate what is good about your business and really over-deliver in those areas – that will win you far more customers than a glossy, polished, generic "same as everybody else" approach.

He has a website, it's not very good, doesn't show half his stock and doesn't even begin to do his business credit but that is really in keeping with what I've been saying!!! (Sorry Bruce!)

Sunday 25th May 2008